Self-Harm

When Abuse Becomes an Inside Job

Dave Ziegler, Ph.D.
Executive Director
Jasper Mountain
Jasper, Oregon

Jasper Mountain
37875 Jasper-Lowell Road
Jasper, OR 97438-9704

E-Mail: davez@jaspermountain.org
Website: www.jaspermountain.org

Cover Design: Michelle Perin
Cover Photo: Michelle Perin

International Standard Book Number: 978-1534683945

JASPER MOUNTAIN
Hope for Children & Families

This book is dedicated to

all those who suffer in silence,

particularly children who know nothing more of

life than pain.

And to all those who attempt to

offer a helping hand and heart.

Acknowledgements

One of the first moral codes that children are taught is often called the Golden Rule—'Treat others the way you want to be treated.' This is very good advice for most children, but not for all. There is an assumption in the Golden Rule that everyone wants to be treated with kindness, fairness, dignity and respect, but working with seriously abused children I learned quickly that not all children have this desire. This book is about the small percentage of the population who start out life being very poorly treated and what can happen to these individuals as a result. Because of the way they think and act, they can be very difficult to understand and therefore to help or even interact with. The place we must begin this journey is to understand that it is most often early maltreatment that has caused this problem, and these individuals deserve to receive what they lacked early in life— understanding and compassion.

Not all individuals who harm themselves in a variety of ways have been seriously abused. This book will not address these individuals to any detailed extent. Instead it will help parents and other family members learn what goes on inside the brain and personality of traumatized individuals with an orientation that defies not only logic, but also instinct. Not all of the book is specific to children, but it is important to understand that traumatized children grow up and become young adults and eventually senior citizens. The trauma from early childhood often is persistent and impactful in the habits and lifestyle choices at all developmental periods. Therefore interventions with adults are in essence targeting the trauma memories from childhood still influencing the adult's brain.

Every day I work with highly skilled and dedicated individuals who have chosen to help children who are caught in the seemingly endless loop of self-harm. These are the staff who work at Jasper Mountain. For many people it is difficult to explain why someone would want a job that includes being the target of disrespect, non-compliance and often aggressive and violent behavior. Not only do many of the direct care staff of Jasper Mountain face these challenges on most working days, but a very high percentage genuinely enjoy their work. For those of you who don't understand this, it actually is not that strange. Research on job satisfaction has a long history of reflecting that money, benefits and status are not the source of the highest levels of job satisfaction. Instead, it is non-materialistic elements of a job that give the employee the greatest rewards. Job elements like doing difficult but important work, seeing your efforts make a difference, working as a team, and doing a job that has meaning and purpose all consistently provide the greatest satisfaction. Clearly most of the staff of Jasper Mountain have learned this, and the children benefit greatly from this group of dedicated individuals. That is the true magic of Jasper Mountain, where everyone wins—the children, their families, the staff, the Board and supporters, and the community as a whole. From the terrible reality that there is child abuse comes the possibility of an organization like Jasper Mountain.

I want to thank everyone involved with Jasper Mountain, the Board of Directors, the staff, the volunteers, the individuals and businesses who support its work, and most of all the children who share their pain, their promise and their lives with us. The Jasper Mountain Board of Directors consists of Rob Morris, Steve Cole, Gary Buss, Cathy Ouellette, Karrie McIntyre, Parke Blundon, Nji Nnamani, Debra Eisert, Barb Lucas, Randy Nawalaniec, Chuck Davis, Gene Heinle and Nathan Lichvarcik. Without this excellent Board of Directors there would be no organization and no success stories.

I also want to thank my wife Joyce who works harder than anyone to make a difference for our children. Thanks to Judy

Littlebury, Michelle Perin, Jim Burkhalter and John Ziegler who helped edit the drafts and offered very helpful suggestions.

Contents

Preface

This is the third in a series of books covering topics that parents, teachers and therapists struggle with every day in their attempts to help difficult children. The first volume, in what is called "The Success Series," covered attachment and bonding problems with children. The second addressed healthy and unhealthy sexual behavior with young people. First things first, why call this "The Success Series"? It is understood that any adult who has the challenge of working with a difficult child will want to succeed in this endeavor. But before delving into the success for the adult, let us start at the beginning and first consider success for the child.

It may seem odd to hear this, but regardless of what you are running into with the child you are working with, the child is currently succeeding, however it is very possible that you are not. Of course, the measure of success for the child is different than it is for the adult. We adults want our children to be successful in social settings and school, developing and keeping true friends, giving and receiving support in the family, and overall reflecting positive emotions that are consistent with living a happy life. However, that is not the measure of success to the difficult child. It may be a bit different for every child, but I have noticed the themes are the same. The child believes he or she wins when the adult loses. Adults lose when they get angry, frustrated and make statements about giving up. Where we want them to fit in well, they want to set themselves apart; we want them to laugh and enjoy life, and they prefer to yell and disrupt any calm they find with a good tantrum. For children we will discuss in this book, we want the young person to experience the good things of life, and often the child chooses pain and suffering instead. In other words, difficult children consider themselves a success when they succeed at what we would consider failing. This is the third of several excursions that we will take together in this series into the thinking of disturbed children.

The reason success for the disturbed child is measured by failure is complicated, but simply stated it is because in the perception of the child what adults consider success is out of reach. There have been dozens, no thousands, of experiences where an adult has made it clear the child will likely never reach the top of the success mountain. The climb is difficult for any child, but what child will attempt to make the journey if he or she has been convinced that the result will simply be more failure? So what I am pointing out is that most adults miss the forest for the trees; they do not see how hard disturbed children work to succeed by their own definition of success.

I stopped telling these children long ago to "work harder" because they were just not putting in enough effort to treat themselves with the love and respect that they deserve. Take a closer look, they may be working harder than anyone to continue to disrupt, to fail, to make it clear to any and all adults that they are unlikely to fit into the mold we want them to fit. Love and respect are currently not on their personal agenda. Consider how much energy it takes to throw a respectable tantrum, or to choose pain over pleasure. Do you remember the last time you 'threw a wobbly' (Australian for tantrum) – not just getting upset, but a fit that registered on the Richter Scale? This would usually mean real anger, some yelling perhaps, even slamming a door or possibly throwing something. Now remember how tiring this was. Difficult children can do this several times a day (some several times an hour), and that takes a lot out of a person. But these children have years of training in preparation for the Olympic Tantrum Team, as soon as it becomes a competitive sport. I realize I am making light of something very serious to most adults, and I am doing so on purpose. Regardless of our challenges in life, if we cannot take an occasional step back to laugh at our situation and ourselves, then the issue has become greater than our ability to manage. When this happens our internal confidence hits dangerously low levels, and we fall into a state some describe as "burnout."

But it is easier to understand a tantruming child than it is to understand self-harm. Consider the last time you experienced ongoing pain and how much energy it takes to live with the pain. There are children who suffer alone in silence, and there are more who wish to share their pain with you, and this is very difficult for any adult to deal with because it feels like the child has all the power.

But my point in starting with how successful disturbed children consider themselves is that most of these children have not given up; they try much harder than adults give them credit. Many have all the makings of a champion, but the drive and energy just goes in the wrong direction. So I am suggesting we start from a place where we see the child as very committed, hard-working, persistent, and a tireless champion at failing in most areas that we consider success. But we must recognize this fact because we will want to redirect this Herculean effort they are investing in their lives. To insure that most of us are on the same page, if you have a depressed, sullen child who does little or nothing, I would still include these children in the self-defined success camp. It is not a natural state for children to expend little external energy, sit in dark rooms and brood. Look at the effort it takes to fight the natural instinct to be interested in the world around them and want the good things available in life. But these children, whom I call the internalizers, (as opposed to the externalizers), must be addressed differently, and can be more challenging than the aggressive and violent children.

So consider that we do not have a child who is a failure, we have a child who is succeeding in all the wrong things. It may take some time before we help the child's brain realize that there is another way to succeed that brings even greater benefits.

Now we can return to the concept of success for adults. We started with some insight that the children I have lived with for decades have taught me that disturbed children do care and do put in considerable effort, and this realization is the start of success for adults. This is because you will not succeed with a disturbed child unless you understand the child, which includes their inner world of contradictory thoughts and feelings.

We adults have a bad habit of measuring our parenting success by how well our children perform on the measures we define as important. For example, the parent of a straight "A" student may have a bumper sticker on their car that appears to acknowledge the child, but before the child is mentioned it says "I am the proud parent of..." Who is really being recognized? Such parents often take pride in their skilled parenting even when their motivated and bright child asks for little academic assistance. However, the parent who night after night works with the math impaired child (an impairment to which I can personally relate) only to see a "C" on the report card, may struggle wondering if they are giving the child enough. I believe it is important to give credit where it is due, and I do not let busy professional parents off the hook just because their child does fine with little help. I also do not hold the parent of a struggling child responsible when the parent is working hard to help, despite the outcome.

We must continue this Success Series with the understanding that to do our best is the best we can do. Therefore, success as a parent is what we do and not what our child does. But let us add to our definition of success to improve our outcomes in preparing a child to have the potential of a future with social connections, with personal goals that are set and accomplished, and with a degree of personal contentment along the way.

We will cover a variety of topics in this Success Series, and each will add to the overall plan. These books will be short, to the point, and are not intended to be exhaustive of the topic. If one of the topics is of great interest, then look into that topic more because there are many helpful resources. Before this series, I rejected the notion of a book on a specific topic because the children I am writing about essentially never have just one problem area. My previous books have been about the whole child, although this theme will be continued in this series, there will be more attention given to a number of specific topics. I still believe that success will only come from treating the total child, and this means addressing multiple problem areas. If you have completed one or more books in the "Success Series" and you find them helpful, then I suggest you consider reading some of my more comprehensive books that have a broader focus on the child. If you are not aware of these books, they are:

Raising Children Who Refuse To Be Raised – This book takes a disarmingly frank approach to the most difficult behaviors and the most challenging children. It not only explains the causes of the most serious problems parents face, but it goes further to provide interventions that have been tried and found successful. Very serious problems such as aggressive, violent, explosive, hyperactive and belligerent behaviors are addressed in a practical and understandable way. Sections of the book are geared directly to parents and other sections to professionals, with a suggestion that everyone read both so adults are working closely together to help these children.

Dave Ziegler

Achieving Success With Impossible Children – This was written for those who work with children who are the most troubled and challenging, and who are exceptions to all the rules. It offers practical applications and hands-on suggestions to help children become healthy, successful individuals. Clearly written and infused with humor, it discusses working with difficult children in multiple settings such as during adoptions, in schools, with parents, and in residential care. It provides advanced intervention ideas, including positive discipline and teaching responsibility. The message of the book is that success with very challenging children is not only possible, but realistically achievable.

Traumatic Experience And The Brain, A Handbook For Understanding And Treating Those Traumatized As Children, Second Edition - This volume details the effects of childhood trauma on the developing brain and describes how early events in life rewire the person's perceptions of self, others and the world. It incorporates two decades of research on the human brain and answers the question, "So now what?" Now that we know a great deal more about how the brain works and how it is affected by trauma, what should we do differently to help traumatized individuals? Case examples help explain in understandable terms how we must work with the human brain and not work against it.

Beyond Healing: The Path To Personal Contentment After Trauma – This book takes a close, critical look at many of our beliefs about human limitations and offers a message of hope for those individuals who have paid such a high price for past abuse and trauma. Drawing on case studies, it provides a clear and realistic guide to reclaiming one's life after traumatizing experiences. The hope offered is based upon science and research, and the writing style is accessible and down-to-earth. This book can be an invaluable guide to anyone who has personally experienced trauma or is attempting to help someone who has.

Neurological Reparative Therapy: A Roadmap To Healing, Resiliency And Well-Being - This book provides a new model of treatment that integrates critically important components of brain functioning this new integrated model is first brain focused (neurological) and stresses the healing (reparative) of adverse impacts that have prevented the brain from reaching its potential, and outlines a roadmap of an active process (therapy) in promoting healing, resiliency and overall well-being. The NRT model relies heavily on the research and professional literature of: brain development, trauma, attachment, and resiliency. The NRT roadmap identifies the best route to well-being through healthy brain development, attachment and resiliency, but relies on the helper to use his or her own skills, experience and techniques to take the journey.

Attachment: The Social Foundation of a Successful Life – No single issue points to success in life as much as the ability to bond with others. Life itself depends upon the ability of a baby to connect with a source of safety, nourishment, and emotional support. But many children do not find the world they are born into a place where their basic needs are met, and they form barriers to connection that can be life-long impediments to success and happiness. This book describes in technical and practical terms what can go wrong in the development of attachment in children and what to do about it. Helping a child to bond and attach to others, despite the vulnerability this entails, may be the single most important step any parent or professional can take to improve the life of a child.

Sexual Issues with Children: Promoting Healthy Rather than Unhealthy Behavior – Sexuality is fundamental to every individual and helps to define our personality, our perceptions of the world around us and informs our behavior. Although sexuality is a defining aspect of every person, it is one of the most stress producing parts of growing up and for parents helping children mature. The job of encouraging healthy sexuality is made more difficult when the very definition of 'sexual health' is elusive, and the modeling of unhealthy sexuality pervades our culture. Promoting healthy sexuality in children begins with taking a look at ourselves because we cannot give to someone else that which we do not possess ourselves. The goal of this book is to help parents model and teach their children acceptance and appreciation of the wonders of sexuality.

I have only one goal for all of the above books— to help you succeed in working with difficult children and to learn from the journey. I have been blessed in my personal life and my professional career to have the very best of teachers, and I want to share what I have learned with you. So let us continue our journey remembering these basic things:

- Disturbed children are highly motivated to succeed in being a failure.
- We must measure our success not by what the child does, but by what we do.
- Our own success will be linked with how well we understand the inner world of the child's thoughts and emotions.
- If we lose our sense of humor at any point in the journey, then parenting a difficult child will simply be a burden, and this will put us on the road to burnout and failure.

Before we continue the journey, I want you to know that you can do this. You can be successful with your difficult child. You may be saying, "How can he say this and mean it? He doesn't know me or my child!" Please consider that I do mean this, and I have worked with and lived with thousands of difficult children, many of whom would surpass your child's level of disturbance. I have also worked with thousands of adults, from those with extensive experience to those with no parenting experience at all, and helped them to be more successful. We know from psychology that two things help reduce the stress of a difficult challenge (and parenting a disturbed child is at the top of the difficult list). The first is having a plan of attack, and I will help you with this. The second is having confidence; if you lack confidence in yourself, for the time being, accept my confidence in you. Now put aside your worry and your stress and apply your energy to fully understanding the problems, and then come up with a plan that will improve your success at helping the children we will be discussing.

Introduction

There is nothing more basic than the drive for self-preservation. Science tells us that all living things have this drive, and it is fundamental to understanding an organism's behavior. This is true except for one science — psychology, that must explain the fact that some individuals seem to act against their own self-preservation and engage in self-harm in a variety of ways. Clearly the prospects of a rewarding life are threatened by the lack of interest in succeeding in positive pursuits. As challenging as life can be, imagine the individual who actively engages in self-harm and what this would do to resiliency and happiness.

The area of self-harm is one more way that humans distinguish themselves in the animal kingdom. Humans are the only animals that intentionally hurt themselves (it is a myth that lemmings rush to the ocean and kill themselves and whales do not beach themselves motivated by self-injury). Why would an animal work against its own best interests? It is only humans who have the capacity to choose good or choose evil, either externally or internally. But we must consider the reversal of the most basic of instincts — self-preservation, as some fundamental level of confusion. Therefore, there is a real opportunity to work with the individual's brain to help it 'come to its senses' and get back to healthy self-care and self-love.

As you will read in this book, not only self-preservation but personal success is the natural state of the human brain. It is therefore tragic that when something so natural is lost, the result can be a threat from within that cannot be escaped by individuals who harm themselves. What begins as tragic can also provide the hope of an antidote to self-harm. Like all human behavior, we must first understand a problem before we intervene in an effective manner.

Understanding human behavior has taken hundreds of years and yet there are still major gaps in our knowledge of human beings. If self-harming behavior was clearly understood, this book would be unnecessary. And yet I am not claiming to have any definitive insight into such a counterintuitive subject. What I do have is the experience of living daily with hundreds of young children who are generally more open and honest than most adults, and they have taught me about their deep internal pain that frequently represents itself in self-abusive behavior. Therefore I do not claim to be an expert on self-harming behaviors, but time and experience has made me an expert on the people, particularly children, who engage in this type of behavior.

This book will begin with the task of taking a very close look at the types of self- harm as well as the underlying causes. We will begin with the topic itself before moving to the specific topic of self-harm among children. This subject is not a pleasant one, and you may need to put this book away at times to get some distance from the world of pain that some individuals are unable to escape. But this is true for all of us who care enough about children and adults who live in a world of suffering that has no pause button other than escapist behavior that is often self-harming. We will see that in many cases self-harm is perceived as actually helping the individual cope with life, and this type of confusion cries out for clarification and help. I have learned from the children I have lived with and worked with that as hopeless as they may consider their lives, there is a deep hunger for a rescuer. Perhaps this hope comes from the recesses of the human brain that knows something is very wrong when pain is pursued and pleasure is avoided. Regardless of where it may come from, the sense of hope that a lifeline may be possible, against all odds, can be the beginning of the healing journey to self-love and a healthy life.

The children we will discuss have also taught me it is very rare that individuals with the internal pain that represents itself in self-harming behavior can find the way out on their own. Rescuing oneself from the internal threats of self-harm is much like expecting a drowning person to find their own resources to move to safety. It may be remotely possible, but not what can be expected. However, unlike the drowning person, many people who self-harm do not cry for help and actually hide their harmful behavior, making our job to help them more difficult.

Without rescue from the helper who will walk into the pain and suffering of the person's inner world, where will hope come from? As helpers, the first resource we provide is our very presence. Individuals who self-harm can tell you how most people are frightened away by the repulsive thought of self-abuse. They don't want to observe it, talk about it, or even think about it. This leaves the sufferer with even more isolation, and nothing hurts worse for human beings than being truly alone.

So I must start by thanking you for reading the following and being willing to endure the unpleasantness of the world of self-harm that we all wish did not exist. But it is when hope comes to the very depths of hopelessness that the greatest good arises. Like water in the desert, bringing hope to the hopeless is life affirming at its pinnacle. And it is also true that the rewards for the helper in reducing the suffering of the person helped has no equal.

Part I: The Impact of Self-Harm on the Life of an Individual

The Many Faces of Self-Harm

It is important to begin our discussion by outlining what is meant by self-harm. There are many possible definitions for self-harming behaviors, but I will offer a working definition. Self-harm can be considered any injury to self that includes physical or psychological components that involves either actions or avoiding actions that are intentional in nature. The reason many definitions exist is because it is rather easy to capture the theme, but the methods are many and often complex.

A close consideration of self-harm is foreign to most people because it is hard to imagine someone intentionally hurting themselves. However, as will soon be clear, the theme of self-harm is actually very prevalent among children, teens and adults of all ages. This issue has as many names as definitions. Some names include: self-inflicted violence or SIV, non-suicidal self-injury or NSSI, para-suicide, self-mutilation, and deliberate self-abuse, to name just a few. Because of the many presentations of this issue, each of these names has a somewhat different emphasis, but all are related. The problem involves three primary themes: 1. Intentional in nature, 2. Causing harm, and 3. Not intended to cause death.

Most people would consider serious self-harm to be rare, but this is not the case. Prevalence studies of young people reflect rates of 12% to 37% of students depending upon the definition of self-harm, and 12% to 20% among young adult populations (Calcedo & Whitlock 2009). Consider a group of ten young people, either one, two or three have in the past or are currently involved in self-harming behavior, and that is a large number of individuals.

Normal vs. Abnormal Self-Harm

Just who engages in self-harm? Initially the topic of people who intentionally do things that cause themselves harm may seem strange and illogical. After all, who would purposely want something bad to happen? Don't we all have enough of that in life? Some may think that anyone who would do something like this must be a little crazy, or at least confused and a bit bizarre. However, before going too far down this line of thinking, consider this—essentially everyone at one time or another is guilty of self-harming behavior. If you think you are the exception and would never intentionally hurt yourself, then stop and think for a moment. Have you ever sabotaged yourself from getting something you wanted? Have you ever made decisions to get less sleep than you know you need? How about chewing your fingernails, eating too many sweets, having more to drink than is good for you, hurting someone you loved, pushing your body beyond its limits, watching more TV than is good for you, or used tobacco in any form? For those with a tendency to judge, may I suggest 'let he who is without sin cast the first stone.'

This book is not about being driven, such as the 'Type A' personality, and ignoring your body's needs, or about typical ways people eat too much. These frequent behaviors can be considered 'normative self-harm' in that most people do some or even all of these things. Our focus is on more extreme examples of self-harm, or behaviors most people would never consider. For example, would you ever intentionally burn yourself or ingest an industrial cleaner on purpose? Certainly most people would do neither.

Let's return to the question of who engages in the more serious types of self-harm.

The common belief that self-injury is a female issue is both correct and possibly overstated. It is true that overall more females than males engage in self-harm. However, approximately a third of self-injury involves males of various ages. Thus it is a problem for both females and males with significant numbers of each. Another stereotype has some truth to it as well, that LGBT (Lesbian, Gay, Bisexual, Transsexual) individuals have higher rates of self-harm. Although self-harm can be found among any demographic, it is more frequently found among gay or bi/trans-sexual individuals. With an understanding of the causes of self-harm, it is logical that non-dominate lifestyles often are correlated with higher stress levels and individuals who feel misunderstood and/or not accepted by others rather than supported by others.

The answer to the question 'how common is self-harm?' is this problem is more common than people may think. Among some demographic groups, self-harm is a factor in 1 out of 3 individuals; other groups have lower rates. Among student populations can be found some of the highest rates, with young adults a close second. However, the highest rates of self-injury can be found among bi-sexual, female, young people. Rates of self-injury among young children are much less known than in older populations, but in this demographic a history of trauma is likely the primary causal factor.

But before we consider the many expressions of self-harm, there are two general categories of these behaviors— externalizing (active) and internalizing (passive). In a general way, the categories of externalizing and internalizing are consistent with the after effects of trauma. Among trauma victims, some broadcast their pain and their emotional distress, while others internalize their pain in quiet personal ways. In the case of self-harm, externalizing is a more active process of something the person does, while internalizing self-harm is more passive and includes what the person should do but does not. The active/passive or externalizing/internalizing categories fit with the brain's coping styles of fight (externalizing) and flight (internalizing). And this is understandable since we will see in detail in Part II that there is often a direct connection between trauma and people who harm themselves.

Suicide—the Most Extreme Self-Harm

The ultimate self-harm is to intentionally end one's life. However, actions intended to cause death are not the focus of our discussion of Non-Suicidal Self-Injury. Suicide is a topic unto itself, yet it is directly related to self-harming behavior. The difference comes down to the goal of the behavior. But further differences in suicidal and non-suicidal self-harm are difficult to separate because self-harming individuals often report suicidal thoughts more than other people and have many more actual suicide attempts or suicidal gestures (Whitlock, Eckenrode, & Silverman, 2006; Muehlenkamp & Gutierrez, 2007; Nock, Joiner, Gordon, Lloyd-Richardson, & Prinstein, 2006; Hawton, Fagg, Simkin, Bale, & Bond, 2000). Additionally, self-harming individuals have six times the likelihood of developing a suicide plan than people who have no self-harming behavior (Whitlock & Knox, 2007). Perhaps the best description of the relationship between suicide and non-suicidal self-injury is that self-harming behavior is an attempt to deal with serious personal difficulties that if not successfully managed may lead to the motivation to terminate one's life through a suicidal act.

Although suicide is not the focus of this book, it will be briefly covered because it represents the most serious category of self-harm. This is not only true due to the finality of completed suicides, which occur on average every 13 minutes somewhere in America, but serious and unsuccessful suicide attempts are even more numerous, taking place every few minutes in our country (American Foundation for the Prevention of Suicide, 2015). Completed suicide is among the top ten causes of death among Americans, with more than 40,000 suicides per year. It surprises some people that older Americans represent the highest rates of suicide, with the 45 to 64 age range having the highest suicide rates followed closely by individuals 85 and older. These older Americans have nearly double the rate of suicide compared with adolescents and young people under 24, but suicide at these younger ages often gets more attention.

Unlike non-suicidal self-injury that is more commonly a female issue, suicide involves many more males than females — nearly four times as many. Another fact that surprises many is that suicide is more prevalent among Caucasians. Whites commit suicide nearly three times more often than Blacks and Latinos. Native Americans have double the suicide rate as other minority groups, but still lower than Caucasians. Therefore, suicide is one societal issue that is not directly related to socioeconomic status or based upon gender inequality. Generally speaking, minorities, young people and females would have less economic opportunity and social status than White adult males, but it is the latter group that has much higher suicides rates. Also, somewhat surprising to some is that suicide is more common in rural, heavily Caucasian states and less common in urban states with higher minority populations.

Two other statistics are of interest. The first is that suicide attempts are estimated by the Center for Disease Control to take place twelve times more often than completed suicides. The second is suicide attempts among the elderly are six times more likely to result in a suicide than among young people (Xu, Kochanek, Murphy & Arias, 2014).

There are similarities in factors behind non-suicidal self-injury and suicide. We will go into detail on self-harm in the next section, but for suicide the following are risk factors:

> A person's physical as well as mental health can be a risk factor
> Serious physical health problems, particularly those that include significant and/or chronic levels of pain
> Chemical dependency and substance abuse
> Depression has one of the highest correlations with suicide
> Mood disorders, including anxiety and Bipolar Disorder
> Behavior disorders such as Conduct Disorder
> Personality disorders such as Borderline or Antisocial
> Schizophrenia

(Bertolote & Fleischmann, 2002)

Research has found that most individuals who died by suicide had recently made contact with a physician or health care provider, but very few had any contact with a mental health provider who could have addressed the mental health concerns leading to suicide (Luoma, Martin & Pearson, 2002).

Additional risk factors come in the form of environmental and background histories. It only makes sense that suicides are more common when the lethal means to end one's life are readily available. More than half of suicides involve guns, and access to guns is associated with higher rates of suicide. Soldiers and police officers are two professions with frequent access to firearms, and both groups have elevated suicide rates. A contributing factor to suicides among soldiers, as well as police officers, can be untreated posttraumatic stress disorder due to traumatic events on the job. Drug overdose suicides are another leading cause of death, and individuals with access to lethal drugs such as doctors, dentists, veterinarians and pharmacists are all among the top ten professions for suicide. Research has found that a significant percentage of suicide attempts are spontaneous due to an acute issue. Therefore, the lack of lethal means at the time could help reduce many suicides (Bohanna & Wang, 2012).

An environmental factor correlated with suicide is the impact of another person's suicide. This can be a factor for young people where self-harm, and even suicide, can be contagious. Copycat behavior is unfortunately a factor when it comes to suicide, particularly among young people. Although somewhat rare, suicide pacts are considered a behavior due to contagion.

Another list of environmental factors includes negative social interactions. These can include all types of harassment. One frequent form of harassment that has received significant attention involves the many forms of bullying, including on social media. There is a correlation between the chronic nature of harassment and bullying that can cause the targeted person to develop an intense need to get away from the problem. If the targeting has gone on for some time, perhaps years, suicide can be a form of flight from this stress. Research has found that this is mostly true for young people with a history of depression. Bullying was not correlated with suicide without co-occurring depression (Klomek et al., 2011). However, if bullying becomes a chronic problem, then it is directly related to depression that can ultimately increase the risk for suicide (Copeland, Angold, Costello & Egger, 2013).

Other environmental factors that can cause sufficient stress to bring up thoughts of suicide are problems with significant relationships. Daily living is filled with a great many stressful experiences, and when these relatively normative stresses become overwhelming for any reason, a lack of the ability to cope can initiate suicidality. Relationship problems are very common for most everyone, but are more chronic and difficult for some individuals. Another relatively common stress involves the loss of a job and unemployment. When such stresses become chronic, then the ability of the individual to cope is directly challenged.

Other life stresses can at times be overwhelming for some individuals who struggle in their lives with a lack of resiliency or the ability to recover after facing a very difficult experience. Death is a part of life, but for some individuals the death of a loved one, a spouse, a child, a close friend or even a beloved pet can produce the experience of being overwhelmed. Divorce can be for some an experience of release and freedom, but for others it can be a type of death with the end of a critically important relationship. Therefore, some of the most stressful events in life are relatively common and are faced by nearly everyone, but not everyone has the capacity to recover from the difficult body blows of living.

Another major area correlated with suicide is past history and background. Although there can be many issues from past history that can play a role in overwhelming an individual, there are four major categories that have been correlated in research with suicide:

- Childhood Trauma and Abuse – this issue is significant among suicidal individuals due to how trauma is processed in the brain. Early childhood trauma, particularly physical abuse and chronic neglect, can produce fundamental damage to an individual's ability to cope as well as producing negative emotional states (Ziegler, 2011). When the stress of daily life is combined with a negative perception of the hopeless or meaningless nature of life, difficult situations can become intolerable situations and suicide can be the perceived last hope for relief. More on the impact of childhood trauma will be covered in Part II.

- Genetics related to mental health problems in previous generations – many mental health conditions have direct genetic links, including but not limited to schizophrenia, bipolar disorder, personality disorders and mood and behavior disorders (Juel-Nielsen & Videbech, 1970; Roy, Segal, Centerwall & Robinette, 1991; Lester, 2002). It is not the mental health challenge that produces suicidal ideation but the inability to cope with a chronic condition. Although there is research looking into the alteration of genetic loading such as epigenetics, up to this point genetics have left many people with chronic and, at times, lifelong mental challenges.

- Suicide of another close or extended family member – there is little question that people can be heavily influenced by the experiences of others. The closer the relationship, the more a person can be influenced. Family members are some of the most influential on many individuals. There is a high correlation between suicide in the family and suicidal issues with other members of the family (de Leo & Heller, 2008).

- Past suicidal behavior – one of the best predictors of future behavior is past behavior. Although not all suicide attempts are motivated by a desire to end one's life, many are. The fact that someone has made a serious attempt to end one's life is a predictor of another suicidal act at a later time in life.

The issue of suicide has been briefly included in this discussion of self-harm because of the similarities between the two. Suicide can also be the end result of repeated non-suicidal self-injury for several reasons, including accidental death related to self-harm and graduating from not intending to cause death to a level of hopelessness that results in now being motivated to end one's life. Three percent of individuals who self-harm will die by suicide. This may seem low, but it is 50 times the rate of those with no history of self-harm. Therefore, self-harm is a risk factor for suicide, particularly if the individual is older, has a significant mental health problem and/or is male.

The most important aspect of suicide is how to prevent it. A good place to begin is to be aware of warning signs of suicide:

- Talking about suicide
- Making statements about feeling hopeless, helpless, or worthless
- A deepening depression
- Dark obsessive thoughts, including dying
- Taking unnecessary risks or exhibiting self-destructive behavior
- Signs of taking steps to seriously self-injure
- Any themes of finality such as eliminating personal possessions
- Acting in unusual ways
- Significant changes in usual thoughts, emotions or behavior
- Themes of saying goodbye such as letters or visits to loved ones

The above warning signs can be serious depending upon the person. The following issues when combined with the warning signs should receive immediate attention:

- Perfectionist personalities
- LGBT individuals
- Individuals with chronic disabilities, particularly young people
- Trauma victims, especially the young
- Genetic factors pointing to suicidal issues
- Parental history of violence, substance abuse, or divorce
- Socially isolated individuals
- Youth with low self-esteem
- Depressed adults and young people
- Students who are reflecting being chronically overwhelmed

Since this book has a focus on children, the issue of Non-Suicidal Self-Injury is much more of an issue with children than suicide. However, it is important to remember that there is a link between these two issues and even without specific intent, some suicide gestures can turn fatal or cause considerably more harm than was intended.

Externalizing Self-Harm

Intentional self-injury can take many forms, and most of these that are somewhat familiar are externalized or outward behavior. These are behaviors that take an active step to cause harm. Here are some of the more well-known externalized harmful behaviors:

Cutting – perhaps most well-known of all forms of self-injury, cutting is the intentional damage to tissue from sharp objects. Cutting is considered an externalizing or active form of self-injury because the individual engages in active behavior with the intent to cause injury.

Self-aggression, hitting and biting – cutting may lead the list but it is not the majority of self-aggression. Hitting oneself in a variety of ways is also a common form of self-harm. This can include striking one's own body or intentionally hitting an arm or leg against another object to cause pain. Biting is also a common form of self-harm. It is particularly common among children who engage in self-aggression. Children (as well as adults) can put bite marks on their hands and arms; at times these bites can draw blood and this may be the goal. Biting can also be internalized harm when it is more subtle and takes place inside the mouth so there is no external sign of the injury.

Risky behaviors – many people engage in risky behavior, but not always for the same reason. Research into this theme has found that different individuals have differing perceptions of acceptable risk, while some have a temperament that craves more stimulation and challenge. In this context, risky behaviors must be motivated by the desire to in some way cause self-harm. This can include not taking reasonable precautions, actively pursuing danger, or any form of going beyond the bounds of safe behavior.

Suicidal behavior – generally there is a definitional difference between suicide and self-harm. In fact, the lack of intention to cause death is often considered part of the definition of self-harm. However, individuals can choose to involve themselves in potentially lethal behaviors with no intention to cause death, but these can cause significant personal harm. Similarly, some self-harm can put the individual in dangerous situations and can even result in unintended serious harm or even death. Examples could include restricting oxygen or taking common and available medications believing they will not cause death (aspirin can be fatal).

Drugs and Huffing – drugs can be more complex than other forms of self-harm because in many cases drugs are viewed by the individual as not harmful but helpful. However, nearly all forms of self-harm are done for a purpose, and most of the time the purpose is perceived by the individual as in some way helping to cope, lower stress and counteract hopelessness. But just as there are many types of drugs that are abused, there are many types of drug abusers. Clearly some individuals view drugs as a way to get through a life that is demanding and painful, but there are others who take drugs with the intention of self-harm.

Huffing or 'sniffing' is inhaling a substance that will cause a response in the brain producing a high or altered state. There are a great many substances that are used for this purpose, and most of them are very dangerous and can produce long-term damage, especially to the brain. Although huffing can be an activity of a wide range of individuals, it is most common among certain populations such as children and teens, low income, depressed communities and environments, disadvantaged minority populations, or all of the above. Part of the reason huffing is frequently found in such groups is due to the availability of low or no cost products such as gasoline, paint, aerosols, glue and permanent markers.

Burning – few nerve receptors signal pain quite like burns. This makes burning a frequent method for those who self-harm. The body must rapidly react to burns, which can quickly cause life threatening consequences. Burns are painful at the time and continue to be painful while healing. This makes burning oneself a ready source of inflicting self-harm and immediately fulfills the person's intentions.

Scratching/Excoriating – removing skin from the body can be very painful which is why it shows up on the list of self-harm behaviors. This type of self-harm was represented in the Oscar winning movie "Black Swan" in a scene that is very hard to watch without wincing. Other behaviors that are related include scrubbing the skin so hard as to produce red welts. Using fingernails to scratch the skin is one type of self-harm.

Excessive exercise – the common view of exercise is not a negative behavior, but it can be. Anoxia is viewed as self-harm and can include seriously excessive levels of activity with the goal to lose weight. Not all excessive exercise includes the goal to lose weight, at times it is the pain and stress exercise puts on the body that is the goal. Exercise has traits similar to other habitual behaviors involving the release of both dopamine and endogenous opioids that can produce a type of addiction. Exercise can be addictive and, even more concerning, it can be a type of self-inflicted harm. Similarly, some extreme and risky sports that often cause injury or can even be life threatening may be a type of self-harm with some individuals.

Ingesting Toxic Substances or Inedible Objects – the purpose of this behavior is to produce bodily discomfort. When children eat objects that are not food this is a condition known as Pica, but usually the motivation is not self-harm. There are many substances of choice to purposefully cause digestive distress and some common ones are bleach, window cleaners and detergents.

Inserting objects into the body – perhaps one of the less known and stranger forms of self-harm is putting objects in body orifices as well as placing objects under skin tissue.

Hair pulling – generally this behavior is included in the list of self-harming behaviors if the goal is the unpleasant sensation of nerves firing when the hair is pulled. When teens and children have a habit of twisting and pulling their own hair, sometimes in their sleep, this is another condition known as Trichotillomania and is generally not done to experience discomfort.

Other Self-harming behavior – there are many behaviors, many addictive, that do harm the person but this is not generally the goal. Behaviors such as smoking, substance abuse of all kinds, and binge eating are very common and close to normative in our culture, but seldom is the goal to cause harm even when it does. However, it does happen that some individuals use these common behaviors for the purpose of self-harm and therefore these issues do make the list.

Internalizing Self-Harm

Other forms of Non-Suicidal Self-Injury (NSSI) are much less obvious and are often done in private and even in secret. These are either what the individual does or does not do with the intent to cause injury. Here are a few examples:

Eating disorders – this type of behavior can have both active and passive components with over-eating and under-eating. Eating disorders are a major topic and can be serious types of mental health disorder.

Depression – also a major topic unto itself, depression is one of the most common forms of mental health problems. All depression is not the same, with some being primarily a type of chemical imbalance, others due to loss, bereavement or major event in life. Depression can even follow an otherwise very positive event such as childbirth. Depression can also become habitual and may form the set point of the person's emotional state.

Self-punishment – included here can be both taking direct action or not doing what the person knows is important for personal care. Direct action may be to directly cause pain or harm to the skin, and not caring for oneself may include not taking a needed medication.

Interfering with the healing of a wound – this could be considered in the category of not doing what your body needs. Although the body will nearly always heal itself, there are many ways to get in the way of this healthy process and cause self-harm in doing so.

Intentional failure such as in families or in school – a more subtle form of internalized self-harm is to take action or inaction to insure failure in activities of daily life. Self-sabotage can take place in school activities, in the work place, with relationships in the family or with friends, and being motivated to prove to oneself that you are not worthy or have little value as a person.

Siena's skin picking was something she seemed unaware of.

At age eight, Siena would pick at her skin so often it had long since become a habit. When she was not actively involved in some other activity, she could be observed constantly pulling skin from her fingers, arms and legs. She did not seem to notice this behavior until she needed something to wipe the blood, and then she seemed surprised with how it happened. Of course her brain was aware that her continual actions to damage her body were the result of her past and her fear of the future, all caused by years of serious abuse in her young life. There was a need to break this habit by providing her with other ways to keep her hands busy rather than habitually causing self-harm.

A Few Facts about Self-Harm

The nature of self-harm goes against what most people consider logical, and there is a considerable lack of understanding about this issue. It is not something people often discuss since the very idea makes people uncomfortable. Because it is seldom a topic of conversation in homes, schools or churches, there is little opportunity to learn more about this issue and to clarify what are often misperceptions. For example, are people who participate in self-harming behaviors a serious risk to themselves or others? Is this problem mainly about people who are seeking negative attention and thus are helped when they are ignored? These and other questions are common thoughts of people when confronted by what most people consider a very strange practice of causing harm to oneself. Since most individuals have never had a detailed conversation about this issue, it is a good place to start by addressing some facts.

Who are the people who engage in self-harm? Although it is fair to say that no demographic group answers this question, it is also accurate to say that twice as many females engage in self-harm as males (Calcedo & Whitlock, 2009). There are likely a number of reasons why more females engage in these behaviors than males. As we will see, self-harm is often experienced by the individual as more of a solution than a problem, and the problem is related to feeling powerless over unpleasant emotional states. Even in our modern world where they have made many gains, females continue to have fewer freedoms and outlets than males; this is particularly the perception of some young women. But there are other groups that make up the population of people who harm themselves.

Like females, gays, lesbians, bisexuals and transsexuals have made some societal gains in recent decades. It is becoming less unusual for a male to call another male his husband. The

United States already has most states recognizing gay marriage. In fact, only 13 states continue to ban the practice which puts them in direct conflict with the June 2015 Supreme Court Ruling allowing gay marriage in the United States (Obergefell v. Hodges, 2015). Now the states that do not recognize gay marriage by constitution, by law or by the initiative process, will have to struggle with the Supreme Court ruling. However, regardless of legal gains, being LGBT in America presents a wide range of pressures not experienced by straight individuals. The result is the second largest population of individuals, after females, who self-harm.

The next population in terms of frequency of self-harm is the prison population. The United States continues to lead the world in the frequency of incarcerating its citizens (Walmsley, 2013). Even with what we have already covered regarding the underlying causes of self-harm, it is not difficult to see that many individuals in jails and prisons will experience the environmental characteristics of powerlessness, depression and feeling unable to change their state of living in an unfeeling and unsupportive world. It is difficult to imagine an environment more suited to hopelessness than long periods of incarceration.

There are other demographic populations where self-harm is not unusual. They include:

- Armed forces veterans who also represent a population where suicide is all too frequent. Unemployment and homelessness are also too common among many veterans.
- Individuals in refugee camps when their refugee status has been extended and shows little sign of changing or improving.

- Those who currently or have in the past experienced physical, emotional or sexual trauma as children. We will cover more on this cause of self-harm in Part II.
- Adolescents when there is a contagion dynamic of young people mimicking or even joining each other in self-harming behavior (Sisask & Värnik, 2012; Bohanna & Wang, 2012; Yip et al., 2012).

Let's return to the questions mentioned above, do individuals who harm themselves present a serious risk to self? The answer is generally no. The answer to the other posed question of whether self-harming individuals present a risk of harm to others is most often no. There are exceptions, but the reason self-harming individuals are not a serious risk is that following some odd logic, experiencing pain is viewed as more of a solution than a problem most of the time. How does this make any sense? It is important to first understand that self-harm is not a problem, it is more of a symptom of other problems, and the behavior itself is most often considered part of the solution rather than part of the problem. This will become clear as we go further into the real problems rather than symptoms. Self-harm is all about the self; therefore these individuals seldom represent a risk of harm to others. Their behavior may create distance, concern and even suspicion from others, but being a risk to others in usually not a factor.

If hurting yourself is not the problem, then what is? There is a constellation of issues that could be considered the cause of self-harming behavior. In general, the goal can be said to be an attempt to alter an undesirable experience or range of experiences. These individuals have an acute, and often chronic, need to stop or change what they are feeling. This can include a wide range of feeling states, possibly including: depression, numbness, distance, feeling lost, unimportance, loneliness, anxiety and many more that will be discussed further in the section, Causes of Self-Harm.

Many people think that people who harm themselves must have a different pain threshold or tolerance than others, but this is not generally the case. It is not that they do not feel pain or feel a different level of pain, because pain is actually a necessary element to change the unwanted feeling state. So self-harming individuals experience real pain and it does not feel good to them and most will readily admit that the pain is in no way enjoyable.

What are the most frequent types of self-harm? Some of the most familiar types of self-harm are cutting oneself, hitting, pulling skin, hair pulling and burning oneself. However, there are many other behaviors that were discussed above.

Is self-harm habit forming or even addictive? The answer is often yes. Humans are habitual creatures, and we tend to repeat behaviors that are either functional in some form or even non-functional. There are chemical reasons that self-harm can be addictive beyond just becoming a habit. The human brain has capacities to produce sophisticated chemical compounds that alter states of experience. One capacity that is well known is the ability of the brain to release chemical analgesics such as opioid compounds that are endogenous, meaning internally released. Self-harm has the potential to cause pain that stimulates the release of these opioids or pain killers. This process can be experienced by the Nucleus Accumbens Septi, or the part of the inner brain that relates addictive behaviors and substances to the brain's reward system of dopamine. Due to this reward system, painful behaviors can be reinforced and habituated. Therefore, even a painful experience can be sought by the individual due to pleasurable brain responses.

Are self-harming people "crazy" in the layman's use of this term? Although out of the norm at least with serious issues of self-harm (everyone engages in some level of self-harm), this behavior is not considered a particular mental illness in itself. There is no diagnostic category for individuals who self-harm. There may be other factors beneath the surface that could be considered mental illness, such as depression or serious anxiety, but this constellation of behaviors is not considered by itself as a mental illness.

What are the future prospects of self-harming individuals? There is some good news with this question: Self-harm is seldom a life-long issue. People change and, more importantly, the feeling states of people change and the causes beneath the surface of these behaviors come and go as do the behaviors. This is not to say that this is just a 'phase someone is going through.' The seriousness of self-harm cannot be minimized by considering it a passing phase, although it could possibly be in some cases. Self-harm is real pain and is caused by real emotional difficulties. It must be taken seriously, but the long-term prognosis is good for most individuals with these behaviors.

Reversal of the Instinct to Seek Pleasure and Avoid Pain

The human body is designed for self-preservation. The nervous system has pain receptors that signal the brain when there is difficulty, and the purpose of this is to try to discontinue what hurts. This system also has receptors that send signals to the brain when positive sensations are encountered, and we refer to these as pleasurable sensations. For the good of the body, humans have an instinctive drive to pursue pleasure and to avoid pain. At times, this instinct can be misused as we are currently seeing in our modern world where pleasure is all too available and pain can be easily avoided. The results can include obesity and addictions, which in a way is an example of an overemphasis on seeking pleasure and avoiding pain.

Some pain in daily life is not only likely, but important. After all, pain is meant to help the individual make every day decisions. For example, when the body is ill and we experience pain such as a headache, stomach pain or achy joints, the individual can take action to address these symptoms and promote healing. On the psychological level, when we 'burn the candle at both ends' by working too many hours and managing too much stress, the associated pain of fatigue and loss of interest in pleasurable activities can signal the individual to make changes in the amount of stress being handled each day.

Mandy was a risk to herself at night.

This seven-year-old managed to do well on most days; it was at night that she had the hardest time and so did her body. She struggled with the dark, and it was late at night that all her memories came back of being sexually abused over an extended period of time. It could have been self-punishment due to her perception of feeling like a bad person or maybe it was her subconscious desire to be less attractive as a form of protection. But whatever the motivation, Mandy would scratch her face until she bled from various places. This was a case where we had to provide very close supervision to protect the child from herself.

While we all have an instinctual drive to seek pleasure and avoid pain, at times this drive can become quite complicated and even confused. Too much of either pain or pleasure is not preferred by the human body. Few individuals desire to sit or lay comfortably for hours or days at a time. If this were preferred, then people in hospitals, rehab centers and even prisons would be some of our most satisfied populations. Lying on a beach sipping a cold drink is the symbol of enjoyment, but only if this is a vacation or a change from normal activity. Many retirees have found that being comfortable and doing nothing is not as pleasurable as they believed it would be, and many look for meaningful things to do. Some very well-to-do individuals who can easily hire others to do their difficult and perhaps painful work, then look for recreational pursuits that involve challenge and no small degree of discomfort and pain. It is the balance of pain and pleasure that best satisfies the human brain.

Another way the instinct of pursuing pleasure and avoiding pain becomes complex is with self-harm. What may on the surface seem to be a reversal of this instinct can actually be a complex extension of the instinct. This can be the case when the psychological pain of every day stress leads the person to initiate painful activities that actually lessen the psychological pain due to the physical pain. This seems more like replacing one pain for another, but to an individual who believes they have little access to anything remotely pleasurable, this replacement is the preferred option to chronic suffering.

However, there are times when an individual confuses the pain and pleasure instinct and may avoid pleasure in many forms, such as the physical pleasure of healthy, nutritious food or the psychological pleasure of having contact with loved ones. At times, some individuals avoid these and other pleasures and pursue pain in various forms. This can include the emotional pain of isolation and becoming distant from others or the physical pain of the many forms of self-harm already discussed. These individuals represent the most concerning type of self-harm. Because people frequently develop habits of behavior and habitual thinking and feeling states, a reversal of the pleasure pain instinct can become the norm and can be a very difficult pattern to break. Some type of professional help is recommended for these individuals. Habitual patterns can be difficult to break, but not impossible.

Children often fit into this category of reversing the instinctual drive to seek pleasure and avoid pain. Some children grow up in unsupportive environments, and they can learn habits from early ages when the child is not aware something is amiss. Some children grow up in abusive and neglectful environments and the child, at least initially, is not aware this is different than it should be. Examples of this can be orphanages in Eastern European countries over the last decades where the child's experience of living is a lack of stimulation and nurturing. In such cases, the environment goes a long way to reverse the instinct of pursuing pleasure and avoiding pain. At times, these children seek to avoid the sameness of a neglectful environment by causing pain in the form of, for example, head banging. In much less extreme cases and those much closer to home, children who learn their emotional and even physical needs are unlikely to be consistently met can develop an internal perception of being unworthy of love and/or lacking worth or value. To these children, self-harm often comes in the form of self-punishment because they mistakenly believe that pain is what they deserve rather than comfort and caring.

Self-Love is the Natural State of the Human Brain

Nature ensures survival of all species by instilling natural behaviors that are self-protective, including survival instincts. Humans may be the only animal that struggles with a desire to self-harm. However, even in the small subset of individuals who face this struggle, the survival instinct is evidenced by the very small number of individuals who intentionally end their life. It is also apparent when considering that the motivation of most self-harm is to help the individual feel better after the initial pain.

For the member of the animal kingdom with the most advanced brains, humans, we can consider self-survival to be a form of self-regard or self-love. In this way self-love is a natural state and is only absent when the natural process is disrupted and confused. We are learning much more from brain research about how the brain is preset to seek positive outcomes in life. This positive state of the brain has been forgotten with all the attention given to mental disorders and ways many people struggle with handling the stresses of living. This can be seen when considering the low percentage of individuals who engage in intentional self-harm and the fact that essentially all self-harming individuals have experienced life conditions that have overridden self-regard and self-love.

The importance of understanding that self-love is a natural state is critical to helping self-harming individuals. If self-harm is an unnatural state, then the goal must be to get the person back to a more natural state of thinking, feelings and behaviors that are consistent with self-love.

Self-Harm Is Often the Product of Environments

Since something must go wrong to cause someone wanting to self-harm, the first place to look for the deeper problem is the environment that produces the stresses that become overwhelming. These conditions are most often abusive or at least lacking the support that mitigates stress. Stress cannot be avoided in life, but stress is far more manageable with a supportive system of individuals and conditions around the person.

When looking for the underlying causes of self-harming behavior, the best place to start is the environment and its impact on the individual. If the source of the debilitating stress and anxiety can be found, then this is a good place to introduce interventions that can turn down the flames of anxiety — if not extinguish them entirely. This is not to say that the cause of the self-harm is the responsibility of other people in the environment. This is an interaction effect —

environmental stress vs. the ability of the individual to manage the stress. There are times that particularly young people have very supportive and nurturing adults in their lives, but still engage in self-harm. This can be particularly true for many adopted children where the environment that has produced the self-harming behaviors is earlier in the child's life and has long ceased to exist except in the limbic brain of the child. These children may experience the abusive or neglectful history as something that is still going on, it is being played over and over in the traumatic memories of the child.

It is essential in cases where the unsupportive environment for a child is in the past, that the current parents realize this and not become reactive due to their own self-doubts. The parents cannot lose hope by assuming their love and support will perhaps never be enough to change the child's emotional set points of depression. A good understanding of the impacts of trauma on the brain can help parents identify the causes and the solutions to some of these problems (Ziegler, 2011). As strong as traumatic memories are, the brain is fundamentally malleable and can learn to get back to natural states of health and accepting love and support when they are available.

Very young children at times self-harm.

The idea that young children hurt themselves intentionally is difficult for many people to believe, but it is a reality. Not all 'clumsy' children who fall often have coordination problems, and not all 'accident prone' children are hurt accidentally. It is very rare for young children to try to end their lives (some do) because the child does not feel he or she even has the ability to do so. Most young children cause self-harm due to rage from abusive environments, and the behavior can show up years after the abuse has stopped. Self-harm is one of many indicators of early childhood abuse.

The Damage of Self-Harm is Much More than Physical Pain

It is important to consider all the negative ramifications of self-harming behavior. A cursory view stops at the impact of the physical harm done by the individual in cutting, burning and other bodily damage. However, physical harm is not the only damage. Just as the stress response cycle, which will be explained in detail in Part II, can over time become a negative and habitual pattern of increasing concern and anxiety, the thoughts and emotions behind the observable self-harming behavior can spiral into a negative pattern of hopelessness. It may be this spiral in extreme cases that leads a person to go from someone who engages in self-harm to someone who becomes actively suicidal, and now seeks to avoid the emotional pain of the anxiety and hopelessness of living by seeking to end their life. The habitual aspect of self-harm, the reversal of the healthy drive to seek pleasure and avoid pain, and the fact that self-harm can be a 'gateway' behavior that can lead to suicidal intent, all demonstrate that this is a serious cry for help that cannot be ignored—particularly among children.

So far the discussion of the impacts of self-harming behavior has been solely on the individual involved. However, in most cases the damage done by self-harm is not restricted to the individual, but impacts all those in the person's life. We will now consider how the presence of self-harm in someone's life impacts relationships with others.

Without Self-love, There is No Love for Others

In considering relationships, we must start with intrinsic issues within an individual who self-injures. We have discussed the instinctual foundation or preset of the human brain for self-survival, self-interest, and success and thriving. This fundamental predisposition is so strong that it takes something significant to override a positive orientation. It takes something significant, but not necessarily unusual. Some of the factors that can override the brain's preset for success, in no particular order, can include:

- Mental health disorder
- Medical injury
- Abuse and neglect
- Living in a war zone or serious lack of safety
- Significant personal loss
- Major life change causing an inability to cope
- Overwhelming stress from any cause

However, the brain's positive default is so strong that even with the above list of factors involved in the human condition, most individuals will get through some or all of the above and endure—and perhaps even increase their capacity for resiliency. This is particularly the case with children, with one exception. Children who at the beginning of life experience a hostile environment and have no alternative life experience to know that living is anything other than pain and suffering. With such children, there is generally a serious or complete lack of self-love. Without self-regard and self-love, the human brain does not consider emotional connection with others to assist with survival because it requires vulnerability. In a scenario of early abuse and/or neglect, self-love can be all but completely absent.

Without self-love, there is no foundation for loving others. Humans are social animals, but how can masses of selfish individuals interact successfully. There appears to be only one way, and that is to understand that social connection returns more back to us than the vulnerability and deference we give others to get along. As Mohandas Ghandi once said,

"Civilization is the art of voluntary renunciation" (Ram Dass, 1979) meaning that for us to get along with each other, we must alter our drive to selfishly ensure that our needs are all that matter. It is difficult to reason with a brain that has experienced no upside to connection with others. If a person's most basic needs have not been the priority of others, there is little or no interest in considering the needs of others.

Only an individual who understands what others can offer will be motivated to give and receive in positive ways. This also requires that a person have self-love and believe they have something of value to offer another person. There is an exception to this principle; it is actually possible to find a person who has self-harming behavior motivated by self-love. In such a case, the individual desires to take a positive step to relieve chronic anxiety and psychological pain. It is not hard to see this as acting out of self-love, although this is stretching the concept considerably. However, most individuals who injure themselves in some way are not motivated by self-love. The majority of individuals who self-harm are acting out of one primary emotional state, and that could generally be called desperation. This is true whether the person is focused on self-punishment or motivated by a desire to reduce psychological anxiety.

Since the strongest antidote to stress is social support, we will see that one of the most potent interventions will involve connections and positive relationship with others. But before this can happen, the potential lack of self-love must be addressed. This brings us to considering what it may be like to be in a relationship with someone who may not have self-love or self-respect.

How Self-Harm Damages Relationships

The damage done by self-harm is not confined to the person hurting him or herself. The suffering caused by this issue to others in the person's life does not get enough attention. In fact, it is quite possible that since self-harm can be a method of coping for the person involved in this behavior, the suffering may be even greater for family and friends.

Relationships are connections with others that represent some element of spending time, energy and interest in the other person's life. Every healthy relationship is based on two or more people giving and receiving from each other. But consider the ramifications when someone in a relationship does not believe they have something of value to offer. When this occurs, the result is often becoming distant or avoiding contact. However, even if one person in the relationship pulls back, this does not mean the other person loses interest. Often it is the opposite, where concern by the other person intensifies as does their attempts to be of help. This is especially true of parents who normally feel responsibility for the health and welfare of the child, including emotional well-being. Yet the dynamic of drawing away by the child and reaching out by the parent can turn into a cycle of escalation, where one person's actions intensify the other's. As many parents and close friends of someone who self-harms have found out, it is extremely difficult to convince the individual that he or she has a great deal to give, and they are loved and valued.

The Golden Rule is one of the main tenants of most spiritual value systems, to treat others as you would have them treat you. However, this principle breaks down with some populations who do not love and care for themselves, and thus lack the first premise of the Golden Rule that you want to be treated well. In the case of individuals who treat themselves poorly, it is not unusual for these people similarly to want others to treat them poorly as well or, at times, to simply leave them alone. These motivations and behaviors are not conducive to a functional relationship.

Most people do not harm themselves and find such behavior, at best, confusing and perhaps even repugnant. For these people, self-respect and self-love are to some degree present and they want to support and care for other people in relationships. However, it is very difficult to want the best for the other person when the person does not share this positive orientation. In these cases, being in such a relationship can be very difficult and painful. Sometimes relationships with people who self-harm cannot be maintained, but most of the time the non-harming person does his or her best to make a one-sided relationship work as well as possible. Ending the relationship entirely or minimizing the interactions with a self-harming person are ways to handle the problem, but these alternatives are not available to the parents or caregivers of children.

So what is a parent or friend of a self-harming individual to do when their efforts to support or care for the person are met with further distancing or perhaps even anger? There are two suggestions in such cases. The first is to do your best to understand the dynamics of self-harm and to realize the causes rarely have anything to do with you. The more you understand the person and the behavior, the more you will be able to cope on a thinking level, while admittedly emotional coping can be another matter. The second thing to do is to ensure that you get the support you need to cope with the fact that you care for someone who, at times, does not care for him or herself. You will be of even less help if you become hopeless and believe things will only get worse and there is nothing you can do about it. There are things you can do and these will be explored.

Regardless of how knowledgeable you become on the issue of self-harm, the fact is that empathetic people hurt when others hurt. But there are examples of pain in someone's life that you cannot change. There are wars, diseases, starvation, accidents, poverty, violent crime and a host of other problems that will likely always be a component of human existence. We all need to cope with the fact that terrible things happen in life and oftentimes to people who don't deserve it. A healthy response is to care, try to understand, and reach out with time and resources within one's capability. However, it helps no one to become depressed when encountering depression, or to become hopeless because there is ample hopelessness in the world. You cannot save someone from drowning by jumping into the water if you cannot swim, nor can you model a hopeful attitude in life unless you remain hopeful. There is good reason to be hopeful when it comes to a person in your life who is involved in self-harm.

But is it a lot to ask to stay hopeful when it comes to someone you love who self-harms? The experience of being unable to stop the behavior can lead to judgment, condemnation, and often anger. None of these responses help the self-harming individual feel better or more hopeful. However, it cannot be ignored that self-harm is one of the most damaging influences on any type of relationship.

Initially, facing self-harm can produce energy from others to do what they can to help. But over time, this energy can turn to resentment and even resignation. When the self-harming behavior decreases or even goes away entirely, as happens in most cases, the traumatic memory of the pain it caused remains in the minds of others and traumatic memories do not go away, they may remain dormant waiting for hints or symptoms of this problem in the future. In this way there is short-term damage self-harm causes to relationships and there is long-term harm as well.

An Internal Working Model That Is Upside Down

In this first section the focus has first been on the many types of self-harm as well as beginning the process of coming to an understanding of this behavior that is perplexing to most people. Demographics have been covered, along with some important facts to counter the erroneous beliefs about this issue. The pleasure principle has been discussed, where most of the time humans seek pleasure and avoid pain. However, there are some exceptions to this principle, and self-harm is one of them. This section will end with a few additional remarks about how self-harm counters the normal drive to want the best for oneself and to act in self-interest.

The concept of the internal working model has previously been mentioned. This is the internal compilation of meaning given to the combination of all sensory input and past experiences forming a perception of self, others and the world. The internal working model is a concept first used by John Bowlby to explain important aspects of attachment theory in children (1982). The internal working model goes beyond the pleasure principle and becomes a fundamental orientation to the experience of understanding living. We have discussed that behavior emanates from emotions that arise out of a person's perceptions of situations and events. These perceptions come from a global orientation that can be considered the internal working model. It is here where the beginnings of self-harming behavior originate.

A healthy internal working model is one where the individual perceives both the positive and negatives of living, with a balance of the two. This includes the perceptions of the self and daily experiences. Not all that goes on in life is positive and enjoyable, and likewise not everything that we know about our self is praiseworthy and complimentary. However, with individuals who self-harm there is nearly always an unhealthy internal working model where the negatives far outweigh the positives in perceptions of the world and perceptions of the self. Living in the world provides challenges for everyone, but in these individuals there is a lack of a core belief that these challenges can be faced and managed with any degree of competency and success.

The issue of an unhealthy internal working model has concluded this section because this concept will be an important component of helping individuals make deeper perceptual changes to overcome emotions of depression and anxiety, and by doing this reducing or eliminating self-harming behavior.

Summary Points

➤ Self-harm is actually a component of self-preservation, but not in a healthy way.

➤ Non-Suicidal Self-Injury (NSSI) is more frequent than most people realize, and that does not include the many 'normative' ways people make poor health decisions.

➤ Most individuals who engage in self-harm fit into one or more of the following: female, elderly, chronic mental health issues, with depression at the top of the list.

➤ Suicidal intent has many similarities with NSSI, except for the goal of ending one's life.

➤ Self-harm comes in many forms: both actions and lack of action designed to cause pain or relief from chronic stress.

➤ Seeking pain and avoiding pleasure is a serious distortion of a healthy personal orientation to life.

➤ Self-love and not self-harm is the natural and healthy predisposition of the human brain.

➤ Environments are major influences over an individual's tendency toward self-harm or self-care.

➤ Self-harm can be a devastating influence on important relationships.

➤ The goal of recovery is to instill a healthy internal working model in the individual.

Part II: Self-Harm in Children

The focus will now turn to self-harm specific to teens and younger children. Many issues that have been addressed with self-harm apply to adults and children, but there are some differences that are important to cover. This part of the discussion will set the stage for preventing and intervening with self-harm and self-injury behaviors by having adults do their best to understand what is behind the behavior—and thus the real problem rather than just the symptoms (observable behaviors) of the problem.

The factors leading to self-harm are somewhat different at every developmental level, from young children, to teens, to adults, and finally to seniors.

- Young children – NSSI with young children is almost always a cry for help and has causes in negative life experiences, particularly early child abuse. Most of the time, young children want the self-harm to be noticed in order to receive help to relieve the stress they experience. Children have a strong instinct to seek assistance, resulting in, at times, extreme attempts to be noticed such as self-harm.
- Teens and young adults – For this age group the seriousness of the behavior and frequency increases. The causes of self-harm are often the same as for young children, but the development of mental health issues such as depression and other mood disorders increases the seriousness of the behavior. For many individuals, the adolescent years are the most stressful time of life. Many factors contribute to this, including the challenge of self-discovery while navigating the very complex and often difficult social networks that teens face. There is less of an instinctive drive to seek help in these years, in part due to the developmental pressure to handle

what life throws at them without always seeking an adult's help. Many more teens and young adults hide their self-harm than do young children. Suicide rates and suicide attempts are much higher for teens than young children.

- Adults – As individuals mature, the issue of chronic stress can increase the likelihood of developing mental health problems such as mood disorders. Like teens and young adults, many adults are covert in their self-harm. Adults above forty years of age represent the highest rates of completed suicide compared to other stages of life.

- Seniors – For some individuals, the last decades of life represent a time of the highest rates of self-contentment in life. At the same time, the difficulties of deteriorating physical and mental health can also produce some of the highest depression rates of any developmental period. The final period of life has its own unique stress when the individual considers that most of their time is past, most of their opportunities have come and gone, and what remains is either a quick or slow deterioration followed by death. Faced with these pressures, it is not difficult to see how depression is high and even normative (most seniors experience some form of depression) during this developmental period.

The focus for Part II will be on the first two ages above — younger children and teens.

Healthy Egocentricity

There are some personality traits that have a negative connotation, when in fact there are developmental periods where the same characteristic is very positive. One of these is egocentricity. Healthy development for children requires an internal high value placed upon the self. The early seeds of egocentricity can later develop into universally regarded positive traits like confidence, self-respect, being self-assured, self-reliance and other traits involved in achieving success in life. Egocentricity is not only positive in a child's development, it is essential. This trait connotes the ability to first identify with the self and second to value the self. However, despite how positive egocentricity is for a young child, nearly all negative references made to this trait refer to teens and adults who have become stuck in egocentricity without considering the value of others.

Egocentricity is a factor when considering self-harm and children. A healthy child will learn that he or she is an individual with thoughts, feelings, and needs and the self is worth reaching out to the world and requesting assistance, consideration and caring. If a child does not perceive the self to be of importance or of value, then there is a good likelihood that personal needs will not be communicated due to believing there is little chance of the need being met. This condition does not eliminate the need; it simply eliminates the hope that it will be met. Under extreme circumstances this can create not only depression in even very young children, but it can also cause hopelessness and even suicidal motivations in children.

There is no question that egocentricity is problematic in teens and adults. When someone only cares about personal needs and preferences and does not acknowledge that there are other perspectives and considerations involved with an issue, it can be like reasoning with a child (actually it is precisely child level thinking). But a healthy child will go through an important period of egocentricity when he or she develops an internal working model of self-value and self-worth. Many traumatized children, particularly after chronic trauma such as neglect, miss this egocentric period and thus do not develop a positive self-perception. It is often from these early developmental deficiencies that self-harming behavior can have its origins.

To not value the self means that it is of little importance to reach out to others, because why would others bother to care enough to listen or respond? Once again, this does not make a need any less potent, but having a need that you believe will not be met creates chronic or toxic stress and anxiety—two fundamental elements in self-harm. Thus, the lack of early egocentric development can result in self-harm further down the developmental path.

It is worth mentioning that when early needs are not met due to chronic abuse such as neglect, this can also create a type of self-centeredness that results in the opposite of what was discussed above. For these individuals, their needs are unmet, become all-consuming and are the only needs that count. It is interesting that this type of unhealthy self-focus can also result in a type of self-harm. However, it will likely be very public and often dramatic because it is designed to gain attention in the only way the individual believes will be effective. This can result in self-injury designed to be obvious and can lead to suicide attempts that are seldom motivated by ending one's life. In extreme cases this dynamic can result in a personality disorder such as narcissism or borderline personality.

Clearly the goal of healthy child rearing is to have a child go through the important developmental period of differentiation of the self, learning self-importance, and perceiving personal needs as important and worth communicating with the hope of them being met. But the individual cannot get stuck in this period and must begin to understand that others must have the opportunity to do the same, with everyone having value and having needs that are important. Those who help raise children (parents, grandparents, teachers, therapists, coaches, etc.) must avoid the two extremes with egocentricity, producing a lack of value, often including depression, on the one hand and aggressive selfishness on the other, and both can have similar causes. It is very common that abused children lack empathy or the ability to acknowledge the needs of others. If a child has not experienced that basic needs will be met by caring adults, then on the road of survival there is only room for one set of needs — one's own. This explains the lack of empathy in many traumatized children.

Healthy egocentricity is the goal and is fundamental to self-love, loving others, and treating others as you would have them treat you. Unless a person has value and personal worth as a part of his or her internal working model, love and caring will be out of reach. Too often the result can be overt or covert self-harm.

Children Who Internalize Their Pain

Most of what has been addressed thus far has been the general issue of self-harm at all ages. The focus will now turn to self-harm with teens and young children. Many adults have a mistaken belief that children are simply small adults, and the field of psychology has in the past made this same mistake. The fact is that children think, feel and behave quite differently than most adults, requiring attention to their unique dynamics. Although children are not simply small adults, they do have some similarities to adults when it comes to self-harm. It is both concerning and unfortunate to see a child engaged in self-harming behavior. Children are supposed to be playful, optimistic and full of promise. Therefore, when a child has developed a state of internal discouragement to the point of self-harm, it is difficult for most adults to understand and it can be very painful for a parent to endure. When faced with a child who is causing self-harm, the first desire of any adult is to just make it stop. However, taking an adaptive behavior away from a child without addressing the causes is to put the child in an even more precarious position. Self-harm can be adaptive when it is done with the motivation to reduce stress, pain and discouragement. Adults must consider what all behavior does for a child or the child can lose one form, albeit negative, of coping.

Most children who harm themselves are adolescents and older teens. As with adults, there are more females than males involved in this behavior. However, as with other concerning behaviors, males more than females may work harder to hide the behavior so there may be more involvement by males than is known. The gender specific message many young males are taught growing up is to be strong and self-reliant. Although these can be positive traits, it takes strength to reach out for help when distressed. We must alter how males are taught so that the definition of strength includes expression of feelings, showing vulnerability and asking for and accepting help when it is needed.

Teen years can be one of the most difficult times in a person's life. Few teens have ideal childhoods, many grow up without the support they need to face an ever changing world that they will have to try to fit into and find their own way. For every new generation in our modern and quickly changing world, many young people believe they can get very little help from their 'old fashioned' parents. Young people think that adults can offer little of relevance because previous generations did not have the same issues and pressures. This has not typically been the case over most of human history when the world the child had to negotiate was substantially similar to previous generations. But things are indeed different now. The pressures teens face are quite different than many of the pressures of the previous generations. For example, most parents have not had to face being the target of bullying on the internet, where hundreds of peers can instantly become involved in cruel targeting. A mean-spirited or even non-malicious tease can now have far ranging consequences and can be devastating to a young person. This is only one of many areas where young people believe, in some cases correctly, that a parent knows little about the pressures of being a teen today.

Because self-harm has its origins deep within the individual's sense of self, it should not be a surprise to find such behavior in the most challenging years of life. Being a teen as well as a young adult is stressful for most individuals growing up. When you consider the external and internal pressures on the person, to expect debilitating anxiety among a portion of teens and young adults only makes logical sense. Internal pressure includes a developing brain that has yet to reach its full potential in higher reasoning centers required for self-understanding, knowing more than information, and knowing how to best apply information or what is considered wisdom. Internal pressures include confusions about identify, about likes and dislikes, about personality traits, beliefs, and fundamental questions of who am I, why am I, and finding a meaningful sense of purpose for one's life. This only touches on a wide range of internal pressures on a young person today.

External pressures not only include the rapidly changing world young people face, but also the need to navigate both one's own difficulties and being influenced by the trials and difficulties of other confused peers trying to find their way at the same time. Teen years are highly social times and often peers are not good role models of health or good judgment. Social media now makes it easy and customary to share one teen's problems with many others. This is one source of the dynamic of contagious self-harm. The social component of teen years is far more complex than at younger ages. Questions always arise not only of who I am, but what others think of me. Am I valued and supported by my parents? To some young people they correctly perceive the answer is a clear 'no,' and others may misconstrue a parent's attempts to help the young person learn discipline, values, rules and structure. Being self-conscious, added to constant correction and negative messages can give a teen the impression of a parent's disdain and embarrassment, rather than love and support. With a brain not fully formed perceptions may be off the mark, but they become the teen's reality.

The myriad sources of internal and external pressure on a young person can be too much for a brain that developmentally is not yet playing with a full deck. Overwhelming anxiety and an intense desire to get some kind of relief from the internal pain can result in external methods of experiencing pain. But not all self-harm among children involves teens; sometimes younger children hurt themselves. Having a younger child exhibit self-harming behaviors can be even more concerning than a teen because life will often get considerably more difficult before it gets easier in later developmental periods of life. Serious self-harm with young children can, at times, be a more serious cry for help than older children. However, supporting young children and coming to their rescue can be easier than for teens and young adults. Young children are supposed to be helped by adults, but teens believe their very need for rescue further represents failure and can increase anxiety. With some young people, this pattern of needing help, being rescued, resulting in more anxiety and demonstrating further concerning behavior can become a negative spiral.

Amelia's early neglect was physically obvious.

Now ten-years-old, Amelia had a deformity that told of her early years. Both of Amelia's parents had low cognitive functioning. She was the victim of extreme neglect, mostly because neither of her parents knew how to care for a young child. As a toddler Amelia had very dry skin on her nose that led to bleeding and scabbing. The irritation led very young Amelia to rub her right nostril area repeatedly, preventing it from healing. Her habit of rubbing the area over months led to the skin being worn away from the right side of her nose. Her parents never noticed the problem, and Amelia now had a face that reflected both her early neglect and her habitual picking at the skin on her face.

Regardless of the possible secondary consequences of rescuing a young person from debilitating anxiety and resulting self-harming behaviors, it is essential to first be of help and then consider the implications afterward. Support is always what is needed for a person who finds the pressures and anxieties of living unbearable.

Motivations that Cause Self-Harm

There are two dimensions of what could be described as causes for self-harming behavior. The first is to consider what the person's goal is or what function does the behavior provide to the individual. The second is to drill deeper to consider what is behind the perceptions and motivations of the person doing the self-harming. These will help show how the root of self-harm often goes back to childhood.

It is somewhat easier to cover the goal or motivation behind self-harming behavior than deeper causes. Although not all self-harm is the same, the goals are usually straightforward. Two major motivations of self-harm will be covered. The first is to alter painful mental and emotional states from a desire to 'make it go away' or to at least provide some degree of respite from a chronic state of anxiety. The second is to inflict suffering due to a mistaken belief that this is what the person deserves for any number of personal reasons.

By far, the most common motivation for self-harm is ironically an attempt to cause pain in order to feel better. It is difficult for many people to understand how cutting, biting, and burning oneself can make the person feel better, but this is precisely the goal of the behavior. There are few pains as difficult to manage, particularly if the pain is chronic, as emotional pain. To use the example of the loss of a loved one, for some people this experience can change a person's experience of the world because such a profound loss changes the brain. As we will see in the interventions section, when the brain changes, the individual's experience of living can change—either for better or worse. Physical pain can often be preferable to emotional pain, and here is where self-harming behaviors give the individual a brief respite from the psychological pain. If the emotional pain is entrenched or very strong, then the amount of physical pain needed may need to be equally significant.

Chronic emotional pain can numb the individual from the more pleasurable aspects of life. Self-harming behavior is often described by the individual as a way to feel again; if not feel good, then to at least feel something other than the emotional pressure and anxiety. While the body normally does not experience physical pain as pleasurable (there are a few exceptions), one type of pain can feel better than another. There is the chemical aspect of the release of opioids that can produce a temporary experience of euphoria and can increase the chances that the behavior will be repeated.

The second motivation of self-harm is to treat the self in the manner it deserves, or in this case disdain, self-loathing or the many ways to inflict punishment. The many methods of doing this are less important here than the straightforward motivation of the behavior. This can be a physical manifestation of self-anger and targeting oneself to change emotional pain into focused action. Therefore, it can give the individual the sense of some control, or at least some level of power over their own life.

The Deeper Causes of Self-Harm

Conscious motivations are not enough to explain self-harm. Behaviors are not as volitional and intentional as many people believe. Behaviors are the outgrowth of perceptual systems in the brain. These thoughts are some of the deepest levels of neuronal activity and are heavily influenced by experience. Perceptions in turn result in emotional responses to the world we perceive. Feelings have little to do with what is going on around us, but a great deal to do with how we perceive the world around us. The same situation can result in opposite behaviors depending upon how we perceive the situation, and this can change from one timeframe to the next. Emotions combined with perception result in observable behavior. Therefore, the self-harm behavior that occurs is heavily influenced by emotions and perceptions.

If you asked someone why they hurt themselves, the person may or may not give you an answer, but seldom will they be consciously aware of the true reason. What you might hear is that the physical pain actually is experienced as relief, or the person feels more alive because of the pain. Few people would be able to give you a full explanation of the influence of perceptions and emotions that may go back to preverbal times in childhood.

To fully understand this dynamic it is important to understand how stress is processed by the brain and the autonomic nervous system. Stress is endemic to being alive and we cannot, nor would we want to, eliminate all or even most stress. Generally stress is our friend; it helps us understand and respond to our environment. It is not always bad; there is also positive stress or eustress. The brain picks up stress from analyzing the millions of sensory inputs that come through the thalamus or gateway of the limbic brain. Stress is usually a signal that attention needs to be given to information coming in. For some people with a history of trauma, stress can be a signal of concern for the welfare of the person. Stress coming through sensory inputs in the brain is recognized by the hypothalamus in the limbic region of the brain. The hypothalamus signals the release of Corticotropin Release Factor (CRF) that signals the two major glands of the body — the pituitary in the mid-brain and the adrenals just above both kidneys. These glands immediately release a number of glucocorticoids, including adrenalin, epinephrine, and cortisol, among others. The job of this 'cocktail' of hormones is to protect the body by initiating the fight or flight response. The body does this by shutting down non-critical systems in the body (for example the digestive or reproductive systems) and diverts blood with its oxygen and fuel to the large muscle groups of the body such as the back, arms and legs. In this way the body is better prepared to face threats by either fighting back or by running away.

But understanding the stress response cycle does not explain self-harming behavior until we go back to the early childhood of the person. Very early in life the brain is on high alert for stress that could result in an early cause of death — the largest threat the human brain faces. Infants and young children experience many stresses as life threatening. The stress response cycle is of little use to a very young child other than one major advantage — the experience of stress allows the child to sound an alarm that is usually crying or screaming. Although the stress response cycle continues to go through the process described above in order to prepare for later in life when it will come in very handy, the young child can take little advantage of the fight or flight response since they can neither fight off a threat or physically get away from the threat.

Philip would ingest dangerous things.

There are often parental warnings on items around the house that an unwitting child might believe is food. These warnings take on a new urgency when a child intentionally wants to eat something believed to be dangerous. Philip was such a child. He had been known to find small pieces of broken glass or plastic and swallow them. He had also ingested the contents of a packet in a box that prevents moisture. The adults around Philip had to be very vigilant to prevent him from causing harm to himself. As you would suspect, Philip had an early traumatic childhood of physical and sexual abuse. His past had to be addressed to prevent him from being a continuing threat to himself.

There is an instinct among humans to respond to the cries and screams of children by coming to their aid. Most adults do not have to be taught to help a baby; the adult naturally picks up the child, cuddles them in a warm embrace, and quietly soothes the child through touch and reassuring sounds such as soft singing. Most of the time this response to the child, in addition to addressing the source of the stress such as heat, cold, hunger, discomfort, etc., soon causes the child to understand the problem is not life threatening and someone will come to meet some basic need. This repeated successful process of perceiving stress, sounding the alarm, and having someone come to the rescue establishes a working memory in the limbic brain. The child experiences some control over stress by signaling for help that predictably arrives, and we call this an early experience of coping.

However, there are children who have a very different experience of the environmental response to their sounding the alarm related to stress. For children in neglectful or unsupportive situations, the child sounds the alarm and learns that either there is no effective response to reduce the stress by meeting whatever the need is, or worse, the response of adults to the child sounding the alarm is apathy causing the child further pain and stress. There is a major difference in the impact to the autonomic nervous system when a parent offers soothing sounds to a child in distress and an angry parent yelling at the child or hitting the child to have them stop crying. The body's response to stress is a cycle because the perception of the brain for the current situation is heavily influenced by what has happened in the past. This is a major reason for the fact that, as terrible as many forms of child abuse are, the most devastating long-term damage comes from neglect. This is because neglect lets the child know rescue is not coming, and the child's brain realizes at young and even older ages the child cannot successfully meet the many basic needs that come up.

So what does all this have to do with self-harm? A great deal as it turns out, because there is a high correlation between individuals who self-harm and those who have an early history of trauma, either abuse or neglect (Brodsky, Cloitre, & Dulit, 1995; van der Kolk, Perry, & Herman, 1991). For the population of individuals who harm themselves, research has found up to 79% have a history of childhood trauma (Low, Jones, MacLeod, Power & Duggan, 2000; van der Kolk,Perry & Herman, (1991). There has been strong research support for childhood sexual abuse resulting in self-harm (Noll, Horowitz, Bonanno, Trickett & Putnam, 2003). Physical abuse in early years has been found to be a cause of later self-harm in other research (Boudewyn & Huser Liam, 1995). Neglect has been identified as another cause of NSSI (Dubo, Zanarini, Lewis & Williams, 1997), as has emotional abuse (Yates, Tracy & Luthar, 2008). In part, what traumatic experience does is to impact the neurological stress response system (Yates, 2007), which can increase stress, reduce the ability to manage and cope with stress, and thus enhance the possibility of self-harming behavior.

Although most individuals do not have many external or conscious memories of their early years, it is quite the contrary with the traumatic memories stored in the limbic brain. Because life threatening stress (and these are perceived to be numerous for very young children) is the most important experience for the brain to remember in order to promote survival, early memories of stress that were not successfully resolved form what is called an internal working model of life. Humans quickly form habits, and when the infant brain experiences repeated and perhaps thousands of unsuccessful stress cycles, the internal model develops that stress is beyond the ability of the individual to manage, and at any time one of them may result in death. This is the basis of toxic stress and produces a deep seated perception that problems come often, they usually get worse rather than better, and rescue is unlikely. The ever increasing amount of stress that is produced becomes chronic, as is the continuous release of cortisol.

Cortisol is very helpful in signaling the fight or flight response, but it has a dark side. Cortisol in high concentrations and/or frequent exposure is lethal to neurons. This is not normally a concern, but for individuals who have continuous negative stress response cycles, cortisol may be ever present in the nervous system of the body—causing damage the entire time. The results can be insidious because there is no immediate noticeable harm, but over time cortisol is impacting not only neurons but also the autoimmune system. Research has now identified that the primary cause of disease in the body is unresolved stress (Felitti et al., 1998). The unfortunate result is the experiences of trauma in early childhood over time break down the body, resulting in the many physical diseases that cause premature death. But long before the chronic impact of unresolved stress and anxiety causes death by physical disease, individuals may be attempting to manage chronic anxiety and negative internal working models of the pain of living by seeking a temporary respite such as self-harming behavior. The pieces of the puzzle can now become clear—early stress, particularly causing trauma from neglect, can represent itself in self-harm later in life (Brodsky, Cloitre & Dulit, 1995). In a similar way, self-harm can be directly linked to other mental health problems such as eating disorders, substance abuse, post-traumatic stress disorder, borderline personality disorder, depression, and anxiety disorders (Yates, 2004).

A final aspect of this discussion of the deeper causes of self-harming behavior is the phenomenon of dissociation. A dissociative state is when the brain experiences a challenge it finds too overwhelming to face and the brain shuts down, much like the nervous system shuts down with overwhelming amounts of physical pain. When the body shuts down both physically and psychologically, this is actually a temporary healthy adaptation to unmanageable stress in the form of physical or emotional pain. However, ongoing dissociation can become habitual. It can lead to a pattern of poor mental functioning and a distant, depressed or hopeless internal perception by the individual of having the inability to manage the challenges of life. Dissociation is most often found in children from neglectful or actively abusive environments because dissociation is a part of the continuum of fight or flight by psychologically fleeing the threat. Once again we see that self-harming behavior is a fabric with many threads: early trauma, dissociation, negative internal working models, poor coping styles, chronic stress and anxiety, and most of the time this all goes back to early childhood years.

Suicide and Children

When stress is overwhelming, social support is lacking or insufficient, and resiliency is mostly absent, the result can be hopelessness in adults and in children. Part I covered suicidal ideation mostly among older teens and adults. The desire to end one's life may not be as prevalent among children as among older adults, but it is all too common and is the 2nd leading cause of death for youth aged 15 to 24, taking approximately 5,000 lives per year. More teenagers and young adults die from suicide than from cancer, heart disease, AIDS, birth defects, stroke, pneumonia, influenza, and chronic lung disease combined (Jason Foundation, 2015).

Before saying more about suicide, I must add that every suicide represents the end of a human life as well as a terrible loss to those left behind. Most everyone has been touched by the pain of someone who has chosen to end their life and thus end their relationships with family, partners, friends and colleagues. I have personally faced the suicide of clients and friends in my own life, and a suicide was the most painful and profound loss I have ever experienced. Therefore, one cannot glibly rattle off statistics without an acknowledgement of the loss and pain represented by each one, particularly the intentional death of a desperately hopeless young person. Preventing suicide takes an understanding of the involved factors, and to do this research can assist.

Research findings concerning suicide and children point out the primary issues. An older study of emergency room intakes over a period of seven years found data on 505 admissions due to suicide attempts. As is true with adults, the younger females outnumbered males 3 to 1, and the males were significantly younger than females. Also similar to adults, the underlying factors included environmental issues such as mental illness, drug and alcohol abuse in the family, family stress and suicide within the extended family. The intakes occurred more often during the winter season. Suicide attempts primarily involved overdose in the hours after school in the home with someone nearby (Garfinkel, Froese & Hood, 1982). This must be considered a sample influenced by the fact that none of the attempts resulted in death. Therefore it makes sense that the means, the setting and the outcome are consistent with Non-Suicidal Self-Injury.

To show that this issue remains similar over time, in a much more recent study the findings were essentially the same. Suicides among young people were mostly males, while suicide attempts were mostly females. Correlations were found to suicide and mood disorders and other mental health problems, as well as significant environmental stress (Beautrais, 2003). Another study on youth suicide found a link with suicide and mood disorders alone or in combination with conduct disorder and/or substance abuse. Once again, completed suicides were primarily males (Shaffer et al., 1996).

Therefore, research over time comes up with very similar results that suicide among children has many of the same themes as suicide among adults—predominantly male, older ages rather than younger ages (seven times more often for youth above 14 than below 14), themes of mental health problems (primarily mood disorders such as depression), and significant environmental stress factors. Also similar to adults, youth suicide has been found to be directly linked with histories of abuse (Shaunesey, Cohen, Plummer & Berman, 1993).

Completed suicides are only the tip of the self-injury iceberg. Studies have found that close to 1 in 5 young people have had serious thoughts of suicide, but most do not act on such thoughts. However, many do and the Centers for Disease Control reports that close to 200,000 young people each year present at hospital emergency rooms due to suicidal behavior. Age is a major factor in youth suicide with teens dying at rates 50 times greater than preteens (Bridge et al., 2015).

Particularly with young people, the focus must be on suicide prevention. Since 80% of completed suicides followed clear warning signs, it is very possible to lower suicides among the young. Risk factors are an important consideration in predicting and preventing suicide; they are similar to adults, but also with subtle differences. Here are risk factors to be aware of:

- Eating disorders of all types
- Substance use and abuse
- Sexual abuse/rape/significant harassment
- Divorce of parents, particularly when this causes financial stress
- Trauma from any number of sources such as accidents, medical issues as well as abuse
- Household financial problems, particularly when chronic
- Being bullied/social rejection/isolation
- Anger/guilt/shame as common emotional states
- Relationship breakup/major loss
- Illness that overwhelms the individual's ability to cope
- Disability that impacts the individual's self-esteem and personal worth
- Domestic violence and/or all types of abuse
- Academic failure in school and grade retention
- Loneliness/hopelessness
- Feelings of being misunderstood
- Insecurities that produce significant anxiety

- Mood disorder, with depression leading the list
- Mental disorders such as Major Depressive Disorder, Bipolar Disorder, Body Dysmorphic Disorder, and Schizophrenia.

As with adults, the ultimate self-injury is when a young person deliberately acts to end his or her life. Suicide is a topic that most adults would rather avoid. Many mistakenly believe that bringing the topic up to a troubled young person may increase the odds of suicidal behavior, but this has not been found to be true. Since the evidence-based treatment for suicidal issues includes a combination of psychotropic medications along with verbal therapies, discussions with young people on this topic are a very good idea, even if difficult for the adult. Like many other issues with young people, ignoring a difficult topic does not make it go away; it may increase the chance of a negative outcome.

The Balance of Selfless Behavior and Selfish Behavior

One of the many reasons that raising a healthy, well-adjusted child is one of the most difficult challenges for an adult is achieving the delicate balance of self-respect and self-love while also teaching respect and love for others. To connect successfully with others requires selfless behavior in a number of ways. We can't have everything our way; at times we have to defer to what someone else prefers. We must weigh our preferences and decisions and their impact on others. Consider toddlers in a sandbox learning this difficult lesson, or how young children handle the experience of attending a birthday party where only one of the children receives all the presents. But too much selfless thinking, emotions and behavior can strip a person of self-worth and personal value. On a deeper level a selfless orientation in life is held in high value in a number of world religions and philosophies. To be nobody special is an important aspect of higher attainment for a Buddhist. At the same time, some spiritual teachers have pointed out that first a person needs to develop the self, nurture the self, love the self, but not get attached to our own self-importance in relation to others and events in life. It was the founder of Buddhism who said that cravings and attachments are the root of all suffering in life (Nanamoli & Bodhi, 1995). Being attached to self-importance or constantly having events in life go the way one prefers can be a continual source of disappointment and personal distress. The balance of self-interests and consideration for others must be the goal of a successful person.

We have discussed egocentricity or what is commonly considered being selfish. However, it was pointed out that what some call selfish behavior is an important aspect of being a successful person. Healthy relationships require a degree of self-focus. Fundamentally, to love someone we must want the best for the beloved, and you must believe you have something of value to offer a love interest. From another paradoxical standpoint, the most selfish thing you can do is to love someone due to what you receive in return. In the same way, to be selfless and to help others is actually very selfish because of the return on your investment. These are more complex considerations than most children (and some adults) can understand. What children need is to learn to care for, and love who they are, and desire to become their very best. This could be one definition of self-love. But children need to be taught, more by example than words, that thinking of others is a critically important part of being a good and successful person.

So parents, teachers and therapists cannot stop with just encouraging a child to consider the self to be of great value. This important first step can be very challenging for many children, particularly those who have had stressful childhoods. Children must be encouraged to learn their value, importance, and worth before they can give these same considerations to another person. And an important part of personal value is self-care and not causing injury or harm to yourself. Children who harm themselves must be helped to either regain this perspective that they have lost or gain it for the very first time.

Meaning and Purpose vs. Self-Harm

As a young person grows up and faces the difficulties and complexities of life, one of the fundamental questions that most individuals consider is the meaning of existence and the point of going through all the painful parts of living. Finding meaning in suffering, in loss and in living day-to-day is something most people struggle with. In research on happiness in life, there are multiple factors that enhance the positive experience of living. These are pleasure, engagement, and meaning and purpose (Schueller & Seligman, 2010). Pleasure has been discussed in the context of pursuing the things that feel good in life and avoiding the things that do not feel good. Pleasure in all forms is one of life's delights. However, as positive as pleasure is, the fact is that it is fleeting and often is over and gone too soon. Engagement also brings more happiness to people and even more than pleasure alone. The more a person invests in a pursuit, the better the chance at a positive return on the investment of time and energy in the form of happiness. However, the greatest factor in achieving happiness is in the area of meaning and purpose.

Meaning can give personal importance and value to many aspects of living, particularly the difficult parts of life. When difficult events happen in life and a person finds meaning in the pain, it can be much more tolerable and the individual may be much more able to cope with the challenge. Meaning and purpose can be very difficult for some teens and young people to find, particularly if their childhood has been marked by trauma. The higher reasoning centers of the brain have not fully developed and many young people do not have the wisdom or capacity to find the answers to the many 'why' questions that come up in living. Why did my kitty get sick and die? Why do I have to share so much with other children? Why do other kids make fun of me? Why did my parents get a divorce? Without meaning and purpose a young person is likely to experience more stress growing up, and depending on the child's ability to cope with the stress, self-harm can become an issue.

The challenge of finding meaning in life is connected to self-harm because of the influence on the stress the individual experiences. Finding meaning can help a person cope with difficulties. Research on happiness has found that individuals who have found meaning through a religious or spiritual system of beliefs are happier than those without this foundation (Lim & Putnam, 2010). Adolescents, in particular, who have found a spiritual path providing meaning are better adjusted and are more able to cope with the inevitable difficulties of living. This in turn lowers stress, depression and hopelessness. Therefore, meaning and purpose can help prevent self-harm in a young person's life. While the lack of a spiritual foundation can hinder a young person from finding meaning and purpose in life, it may not be called a major cause of self-harm. However, having meaning and purpose can be an important resiliency factor and is associated with better coping and overall happiness (Holder, Coleman & Wallace, 2008).

The fundamental components of behavior start with perceptions. What we perceive in life is directly impacted by the meaning that we affix to our experiences. The expression 'change your thinking, change your life' (Tracy, 2003) is actually an idea that has been around a very long time. One of the quickest ways to improve one's life, lower stress, and improve mood is to change the way we perceive our situation. The healthiest individuals are those who invest in improving mind, body and spirit. Although often considered a spiritual concept, meaning and purpose impacts all areas of the self. Feeling connected to something greater than the self—such as family, community, social network, team, church, job, etc.—is a recipe for a healthier mood without depression and therefore a means to prevent or reduce the stress that can cause self-harm. Not only can meaning and purpose reduce stress, but it can also improve happiness and personal contentment. There is a lot to like about improving one's life by enhancing pleasure, engagement and finding more meaning and purpose.

Understanding the Behavior of Children

The primary concern of any adult when it comes to self-harming behavior with a young person is to prevent or to successfully intervene with all forms of self-injury. Part III will consider specific methods to intervene with NSSI. But before adults can successfully intervene, the first step is to understand confusing behavior that seems to make no logical sense. To understand a specific behavior, it is helpful to take a step back and consider how to understand overall behavior in children, particularly those with traumatic backgrounds.

Many adults do not understand the behavior of children because they think children are just small adults in their outlook and thinking, and in most areas this is not accurate nor helpful. These adults will project onto the young person their own perceptions and motivations, which is a type of transference (consciously or unconsciously believing another person thinks and feels as you do). The problem is that unless the adult has a background of struggling with self-harm, he or she is likely to misunderstand the child. Children are not just small adults primarily because of brain development. There are stages of brain development that begin before birth and reach a developmental milestone around the mid-twenties (full development of ethical, moral and altruistic reasoning). However, one must use caution when giving timeframes of development because everyone is different. The brain continues to adjust and change throughout life, but at different rates and degrees for different individuals. Usually by the mid-twenties, most individuals have reached the capacity to use their highest forms of reasoning that will continue to be altered throughout the person's life based upon experience.

If children are different than adults, then how can their behavior be best understood? After all, adults were once children, but for many reasons, including the changing brain, it is difficult for adults to remember their reasoning at each developmental period. I was reminded of this recently when I looked at a toy catalog. Memories immediately came back of being a young boy when before Christmas I would look at the Sears Catalog and go page by page looking at all the fascinating toys. Although I remember my feelings of wonder and excitement with these toys, looking at similar toys today I don't quite understand what the excitement was all about. The brain stores enormous amounts of memory but not all memories are the same, and we tend to remember experiences (for example tastes, smells and sounds, particularly music) and feelings much more than our early thoughts and reasoning. So my memories are of how I felt about toys and the approaching holidays, but my thinking at that age is no longer clear.

The place to start in understanding the behavior of children, and ultimately self-harming behavior, is with what behaviors represent. Several decades ago the standard in psychology was behaviorism. If you wanted to be taken seriously in psychological circles, you had to have a full understanding of, and explain yourself in, behavioral language. But the more human behavior was studied, the limits of behaviorism became clear (although some behaviorists remain true believers today). Behavior was an outgrowth of something else, and what took the place of behaviorism became cognitive behavioral principles that recognized that thoughts result in behaviors. However, a more in-depth look at behavior will easily show that thinking (perceptions) are very important, and so are the emotional reactions connected to and following perceptions. Therefore, to fully understand the behavior of children, we need the formula $P + E = B$ or perceptions combined with the emotions elicited produce what we observe in behavior.

To further break this down, consider that behaviors are the outgrowth of perceptions and how the individual subjectively views and understands a situation. Based upon this subjective perception, the individual will develop an emotional response. It is therefore not what the objective reality happens to be for a child, but the perception of the reality that produces a range of emotional responses. An example of this is when there are two cupcakes and two children, with both children getting one cupcake. However, whether accurate or not, if one child perceives that the other cupcake is a fraction larger than his cupcake, this can create a negative emotional response. Take the same two children with only one cupcake that is divided between them, and the same child believes his share is a bit larger than the other child's share and this can produce emotional satisfaction. So the reality, that the child received more cake in the first scenario but was unhappy and less cake in the second scenario and was happier, points out that it is not what happened, but how the child perceived what happened that produced the response. By the way, this is one of the areas where children and adults respond very similarly, just replace the cupcake for _____ (fill in the blank) and watch how many adults respond to their perceptions rather than the objective reality.

There is another complex factor that will be mentioned briefly in how the brain perceives a situation and that is past experience. Perceptions are a complex outgrowth of billions of synaptic neuronal connections that are heavily influenced by how the brain understands current reality compared to memories of past experience. In other words, what has happened in the past shapes our experience of what happens in the future. For some this can be positive, but for traumatized children the past often preconditions the child for a negative outlook or negative 'internal working model.' When memories, particularly the impact of traumatic experiences, come into the equation to produce perceptions, we adjust our formula with behavior being $P + TM + E = B$ or perceptions are influenced by memory, particularly traumatic memory, resulting in emotions, and the observable outcome is the behavior we see.

Adults are not expected to be psychologists or experts in the behavior of children, but to be an effective parent, particularly of a child who struggles with NSSI, it helps to be an expert in your own child's behavior. However, what most adults do is get in a hurry and skip the most important steps to understand a child's behavior. This happens when an adult sees problem behavior and misconstrues the symptom for the underlying problem. In these cases the adult is most likely to come up with ineffective interventions because the focus is on the symptom rather than the actual problem.

To use a somewhat humorous example (most examples are not so humorous), when my younger brother was 4 years of age, like most children he had some trouble regulating himself at times. Once we were catching bees in a field of flowers and my brother had been corrected by my father several times to calm down. All of a sudden he began to jump around and create a commotion. My father had had enough of his antics and swatted him on the rear end (a common intervention in the 1950s). The result was to send my brother into hysterics with screaming and flailing. Only when my mother finally heard why my brother was screaming did his behavior improve. My father thought the problem was my brother's lack of self-control, however, the underlying problem was the bee that had flown up the leg of his shorts! Bee removed, real problem resolved, behavior improved. Obviously the swat on the rear did not help matters and instead made the situation considerably worse, for both the bee and my poor brother. If adults get in a hurry, assume they immediately know the problem and step in with the first intervention that comes to mind, the results can be anything from ineffective to disastrous, and seldom will the outcome have the desired consequence.

In working with significantly traumatized children for many years, the concept of 'translating' has been used to help understand childhood behavior. Translating behavior is to take a moment to consider the meaning of the behavior to the child. Children differ in how they view situations, and taking the time to understand what this child is demonstrating with this specific behavior will bring new and important information. A good way to translate behavior is to consider several possible meanings. What is the child saying through this behavior? Then do your best to identify the most likely translation. You could in fact be incorrect, and if so you will need to revise your translations when your intervention does not produce the desired results. The more adults translate the behavior of the child, the better they become at understanding behavioral problems. It is not only the practice that produces the improvement, but also the fact that the adult puts aside adult thinking to consider the meaning of the behavior based upon this child's perceptions.

A number of years ago a therapist I supervised was working with a child with selective mutism (although she was able to speak, she chose not to). The therapist asked me in supervision how she was supposed to find out anything about the child's inner world since the young girl just sat and said nothing in their time together. My response was to tell the therapist that this was actually a blessing to help her learn important therapy skills. Children often use words to say the opposite of what they really mean. As adults we must learn to understand the child's internal working model, their internal perceptions and motivations behind the behavior. However, with many traumatized children, language is often used as a form of self-protection—such as wish fulfillment, hoping what they say will come true, confusing adults from what is really going on, and as an attempt to keep adults at a distance. Children use language for many reasons, but not always to communicate their actual meaning. It is helpful when considering the words of a child with a trauma background to first consider the opposite of what they say to determine if the opposite might be much closer to the child's real message.

Traumatized children often speak in opposites.

The goal of most traumatized children is to eliminate as much vulnerability as they can. Past experiences of being hurt result in not wanting to be understood or not wanting to rely on others whenever possible. When others know us well we are vulnerable; when others see our needs we are vulnerable. For traumatized children language becomes a way to protect themselves. Consider the following:

I am not sad that my mother died.	I am not only sad but scared.
I don't need you or anyone.	I can't make it alone but who can I trust?
I hate this adoptive family.	I am scared that I feel like I belong here.
You are the worst teacher ever.	I might start liking school because of you.
I can do it. I just don't want to.	I wish I could but I know I will fail again.

Before taking the first statement at face value, consider the opposite and then ask yourself which is likely to be the real message from the child. Anger often hides fear and sadness, and pushing adults away is preferable to being rejected once again.

In Part III we will use the formula $P + TM + E = B$ as well as the concept of translating to better understand behavior and put it into some scenarios to show how the behavior of difficult children can be understood. The adult can then take steps to increase the odds that interventions have the best chance at success.

The Dark Inner World of Self Abuse—A Cry for Help

Not all self-harm is a cry for help. Many individuals who self-injure do so in private and do their best to conceal their actions. This is due to the stigma and embarrassment they feel. They believe they would be looked down upon by others, and thus actually increase the stress and pain they feel. However, concealing self-harm occurs much more often with older teens and adults and is unusual for young children. For children self-harm is nearly always a frantic cry for help.

A dynamic related to self-harm occurs with children who have experienced significant abuse and/or neglect that is brain-based. When a young child is forming an internal working model and experiences a message from the environment that indicates the child is not of high value, this is internalized and can have long-lasting and significant consequences. This dynamic forms low self-esteem and can lead to self-harm. An internal working model of low personal value is also a principle reason why neglect has the most profound long-term impacts of any type of child abuse on an individual.

As a child matures, a negative internal working model defines much of the child's perceptions. However, there are other messages that the brain picks up from observing other adults and children, and soon the child begins to get the message that something has gone terribly wrong in their upbringing. At this point the formula of developing behavior can be used once again where $P + TM + E = B$, perception + traumatic memory + emotions = behavior. The child develops perceptions of low worth, combined with traumatic memories of negative experiences, resulting in feelings such as anger or depression (fight or flight) that will produce behaviors related to these negative feeling states (external aggression or internalize aggression). In many ways the children who externalize their anger represent a population that is easier to help than internalizing children — in part because one form of internal aggression is self-harm. Externalized aggression is easier to work with because it is more overt, easier to understand and you usually get instant feedback as to whether your interventions have worked.

Young children usually do not hide their self-harm as many teens and adults do, because children are more reactive and less thoughtful. Another reason is that when a child has a sense that something is wrong with how they have been treated growing up (abuse/neglect), the internal working model tells the child he or she is of low personal worth, but the child rebels forming an internal conflict as well as externalized behavior indicating struggle and conflict. It is of little use to sound the alarm with self-harming behavior if this is done covertly and others are not aware that the child needs support and needs to be rescued from the internalized hopelessness and depression.

The default of the human brain is to promote survival of the individual, but also to promote thriving (Ziegler, 2011). Child abuse and neglect, as well as other types of trauma, can reset the brain to a primary focus on survival and attempting to control as much of their life as possible. When survival is experienced as an active struggle, this is to the detriment of important developmental priorities such as having fun, learning, exploring their environment and seeking positive attention and support from adults. However, there is still an internal conflict between surviving and thriving. The conflict for the child is a desire to be controlling, reactive, and unwilling to be vulnerable, while knowing they are pushing away the very adults who may be of support and while the child's instincts are to seek safety, support, comfort, and caring. All this internal conflict results in chronic stress, the continual release of cortisol and, at times, the need to self-harm for momentary relief from the stress and pain they experience. Young children instinctively know to cry out for help, but due to the negative internal working model, the child is not confident their cry for help will be successful. This dynamic of crying out but not trusting the response results in the challenge faced by parents of self-harming children.

Some children resolve the internal conflict explained above by essentially giving up on the hope of being helped or rescued. These children learn to bear their pain internally, at times, self-blaming for being unlovable and not being worthy of having a better life than they have thus far experienced. This can come from some of the more serious and chronic types of trauma such as ongoing sexual abuse or chronic and brutal physical abuse. One aspect of these terrible types of child abuse is that the same adults the child must rely on for protection are the very source of threat to the child's well-being. These types of trauma have been called 'the ultimate betrayal' and for good reason. In these cases, even young children can become internalizing in their self-harm by focusing their anger and aggression on him or herself. As previously mentioned, these can be some of the most challenging children to help because they have lost the belief that there is a chance of rescue or a better life available to them. Many times these children will self-harm because it is preferable to being harmed by someone else, in this way the child experiences at least a small amount of control. This is a tragic choice since the child perceives there will be pain and suffering one way or the other, and such perceptions will result in some level of hopelessness. When a child essentially gives up hope, the ability to care even for oneself can be seriously damaged or even lost. These children can engage in risky behavior which some adults misperceive as being 'accident prone,' but there may be no accident involved. These children can also develop many of the types of self-harm discussed in Part I. If the child has little or no hope of things changing, then their next terrible choice is to endure their anxiety and pain silently or consider suicide.

Head banging is a common form of self-harm for young children.

Many parents have experienced their child get so frustrated that they bang their head on the floor or a wall. Most of the time this is not an attempt to cause harm, but an outward statement of frustration and is often designed to get something the child was not allowed to have. However, some children who have histories of early trauma will hit their head on very hard surfaces and with enough force to cause damage. This is one of many symptoms of previous childhood physical abuse, and the goal is to cause harm. The child is demonstrating that he or she sees life as a place of pain whether coming from the outside or from within. This behavior is unlikely to change without interventions targeting the child's perceptions and feelings about their world.

Understanding the Risks

The distinction between NSSI and suicide is not as definitive as it would seem. In fact, the similarities are so close that the only fundamental difference is in the desired outcome where one act is designed to result in death and the other does not. However, this does not account for motivation because in some suicides the motive was not to end in death, and in some suicide attempts the desire to end in death was not attained. Therefore, it is neither possible nor helpful to conclude that NSSI is of little meaningful risk, all self-harm holds risk.

One risk of non-suicidal self-harm is the development of chronically poor health habits. There is unnecessary stress that is placed on the body's immune system with habitual behaviors such as cuts, burns, and placing foreign objects under the skin. Other behaviors such as ingesting non-food liquids can cause damage to the digestive system and sensitive tissue. Clearly harming the body in intentional ways will over time create risks of damage that would not be present otherwise. The risks are greater for young children who are developing health habits that can continue throughout life. If these habits are intentionally poor, there can be long-term risks to the health of the individual.

Even when self-harm is not intended to create serious damage or death, habitual self-harm increases the risk of suicide 50 times greater than individuals who do not engage in self-harm. Neither self-harm nor suicidal ideation necessarily occur in isolation. There is a higher risk of both self-harm and of suicidal themes in families where these behaviors are present (de Leo & Heller, 2008). Therefore, non-supportive families or the absence of nurture must be added to the list of risks.

Fortunately, the statistics point to the favorable conclusion that the vast majority of self-harming behaviors do not end in death. Even for overt suicide attempts, some populations have 99% non-lethal outcomes for every suicide (young children and female teens). However, other populations have death rates several times this high (middle aged males and the elderly). All self-harm involves a level of risk and should always be taken seriously.

What Research Says about Individuals Who Live with Trauma, Depression and Chronic Anxiety

Before moving to the most important section covering what can be done to prevent and intervene with individuals who self-harm, there is one additional major risk factor that is directly related to the causes of self-harming behavior — the increased chance of preventable medical disease that can even include an early death.

Nearly two decades ago, a large Health Maintenance Organization in Southern California embarked on a large scale study to determine the root causes of disease and to learn if health habits could not only improve the quality of life but also extend life. The study initiated by Kaiser Permanente was joined by the Centers for Disease Control and resulted in the largest epidemiological study in US history. To report the complex results in simple terms, the research investigators found to their complete surprise that the top ten causes of preventable death in the United States came down to chronic stress from early life trauma. The physicians who were the lead investigators had not considered such a result. They immediately began a decades long closer look into the trajectory of early overwhelming stress, that later in life could produce a break down in the immune system and the body's ability to be resilient when encountering disease. Could it be possible that such conditions as: heart disease, chronic obstructive pulmonary disease, cancer and all major causes of death in the United States were actually caused by traumatic experiences early in a person's life? The initial results and all subsequent replications of the study have now shown a definitive affirmative answer to this question (Felitti et. al., 1998).

The impacts of chronic or toxic stress are now very well known, due in no small part to the Adverse Childhood Experiences (ACE) studies. The initial findings pointed to a statistically significant correlation between physical disease and early experiences of trauma. The researchers considered ten types of early trauma in childhood and then considered any link with serious medical problems later in life. Regardless of how the data was analyzed the results were remarkably consistent. Each time the findings indicated that early trauma resulted in medical disease. Early trauma included: emotional abuse, physical abuse, sexual abuse, neglect, abandonment, domestic violence, substance abuse, a caretaker with a mental illness and criminal incarceration. When each of these risk factors was considered with later medical illness and disease, there was a 1 to 1 correlation.

The initial ACE study was expanded multiple times to consider other serious dysfunction later in life with identical findings. In addition to medical disease, correlations were also found between early childhood trauma and substance abuse, obesity, and underemployment, to name a few. With each study the message became stronger—the best way to prevent a long list of future problems in life was to do something about early trauma and how the body handles chronic stress. Not only have the ACE studies increased the urgency to prevent child abuse and early trauma, they have also pointed to the need for radically different approaches to medical care at different stages of life.

The implications of early trauma, chronic stress and emotional states of depression, anxiety and related mental health disorders are clearly reflected in the ACE studies over the last fifteen years of research. The findings have been repeatedly replicated that the body's struggle with stress caused by emotional and psychological states such as depression and anxiety not only are major factors that cause self-harm, but they are also causal factors in medical illness and terminal disease. This puts the need to reduce the causes of self-harm in even greater focus because it is the same dynamic, reviewed previously in the discussion of the stress response cycle, that is behind self-harm and behind physical disease that can shorten life.

Self-Harm is Not Always Obvious with Children and Teens

One of the last things a parent wants to consider is a child so unhappy that he or she is resorting to self-harm. While much of the time self-harm is easily identified, this is not always the case. There are many 'normal' harmful events in a young person's life—injuries, accidental overdoses, risky behavior, reckless driving, and for young children ingesting poison, clumsy behavior resulting in injury and being 'accident prone.' While most of the times these forms of harm are what they appear to be, some turn out to be intentional self-harm. Similar to the above discussion of translating a child's behavior, it is worthwhile to stop and consider what may be behind behavior that results in harm to a child, particularly if harm is a frequent outcome. Not all accidents are what they appear to be. Unless an adult is able to determine if a child intentionally is self-harming, then the child will not get the help they may desperately need.

We will now turn our attention in Part III to what adults can do to prevent and intervene with self-harm by children.

Summary Points

➤ Egocentricity is a healthy and important aspect of early development of a positive sense of self.

➤ Teens engage in self-harm much more often than young children, therefore, self-injury with young children may indicate an increased degree of concern.

➤ The two important questions to ask about self-harm are 1. What is the motivation of the child? and 2. What are the deeper causes of the behavior?

➤ Ongoing stress from early traumatic experience is a leading cause of self-harm. If coping skills are not learned early, the result can be life-long toxic stress that can cause physical disease.

➤ Suicidal ideation is much more common in teens than young children and should always be taken seriously.

➤ Depression and other mood disorders are closely correlated with both self-harm and suicidal thoughts and behavior.

➤ Self-injury of all types is an indication of a lack of self-love.

➤ Understanding the cause of a child's behavior is very important before intervening when self-harm presents itself.

➤ The formula to understand a child's behavior is perceptions plus traumatic memory along with emotional states results in the behavior we see, or $P + TM + E = B$.

- ➤ Children who self-harm must rely on adults to be rescued.
- ➤ Self-harm can lead to later suicidal acts if the cry for help has not been recognized.
- ➤ The same causes of self-harm also can cause chronic life-long stress, resulting in serious medical conditions later in life as well as premature death.
- ➤ Self-harm with children may not always be obvious.

Part III: Impacting the Thinking and the Behavior of Children Who Harm Themselves

At this point in our discussion a number of things should be clear: self-harm is serious even if it may start out in minor acts, self-harm is a concern for all ages and children should lead the list, without intervention self-harm can turn into suicidal themes and the child or teen may not have the ability or self-understanding to improve the situation he or she is in. For these and many other reasons, including our sense of obligation, the solutions are left up to knowledgeable and concerned adults to help young people with acts of self-harm.

No information on this topic would be complete without putting a focus on what can be done to help eliminate NSSI. This final section will address what concerned adults can do to help.

Self-Harm Can Be Addictive

Thus far the case has been made that self-harming behavior should be of concern to the adults in the child's life and not what some adults think, such as 'it is just a phase she is going through' or 'he just wants attention.' In addition to the other reasons to take self-harm seriously, there is one more that will be mentioned. Human behaviors that are repeated can become habituated, whether healthy or unhealthy. In part, this is because of the way the human brain operates.

The brain places a priority on efficiency. It is the most complex of organs, and it cannot afford to invest the necessary resources that it takes to choose a complex route when a simple path is possible. Brain cells called neurons are some of the most vulnerable cells in the body. Without sufficient oxygen and fuel (glucose), a neuron will die within minutes. This is a serious matter to have such vulnerable cells that with proper care can live for 80-100 years. This is why a stroke is so serious. When blood is prevented from getting to brain cells for any period of time, the result will usually be the death of huge numbers of neurons, and this can cause devastating impacts on many of the brain's functions, such as: speech, motor control, and even consciousness and life itself. Therefore, the brain looks for efficient ways to control the hundreds of bodily systems it regulates. Efficiency requires that the job get done with the minimum amount of neurological effort.

What requires the least amount of thinking and reasoning becomes the priority for the brain. This is where habitual behavior becomes important. Consider the last time you drove on your familiar daily commute only to reach your work place before you realized it—because you were planning your morning. Your brain was handling the many thousands of decisions related to estimating distances, monitoring speed, considering the right speed to go around corners, what lane to merge into with heavy traffic, and all while you were thinking about something else. The brain was relying on habits formed over years of operating a vehicle. To use another example, here is an experiment—tomorrow morning consciously decide to take your shower and wash your body differently than ever before. Watch how much effort this takes rather than what nearly everyone does day after day and year after year—washing yourself in the very same way. When we employ habits, we save mental energy so it can be used in more important matters, like planning an important meeting while taking the shower or driving to work.

The brain develops efficient and habitual behaviors starting early in life. The behaviors that turn out to be functional will likely become long-term habits. What parents and other adults need to protect against is a young child finding a functional method to handle stress and difficulty in life that turns out to be unhealthy, such as overeating, dissociating, or NSSI. The earlier in life the habit forms, the more the brain will rely on the easiest and most familiar path to accomplish the goal. Self-harm can be a devastating habitual behavior, and some children resort to it the same as with other habits—without giving it any thought, which is precisely the goal of a habit.

Habits are formed first for efficiency and then following the mathematics of repetition, that the more a behavior is repeated, the more likely it is to be replicated. Young children can develop long-term habitual problem behaviors at times without even being aware they are doing it. The issue of habitual behavior begins our discussion of preventing self-harm because early intervention can prevent years of unhealthy habitual behavior in the future. The goal is to use the same brain mechanisms (efficiency, habit and repetition) to turn an unhealthy habitual behavior into a healthy coping behavior. Doing so can put a halt to a problem behavior before it becomes a serious habit, and can reinforce a positive coping behavior in its place that will be strengthened as it is repeated.

Self-Harm Is the Brain Tricking Itself

Regardless of how habitual self-harming behavior is for a young person, there is a problem in how the brain processes the behavior. When the individual's autonomic nervous system responds to self-harm by reducing the amount of overwhelming stress, the reasoning centers of the brain perceive that something positive has happened and there will be an incentive to repeat the behavior. If the behavior in question is NSSI, the brain will fool itself into believing something harmful is actually something helpful.

Since the brain puts a priority on behavior it considers helpful, there are other factors that give this signal to the brain producing a tendency to repeat the behavior in the future. The child can experience some perceived positive results from what most people would consider a negative behavior like self-harm. The following are part of this perception of positive factors:

❖ **Letting your behavior tell your story** – many children struggle with communicating difficult feeling states. This is particularly true with negative feelings like sadness, depression and hopelessness. These are difficult feelings even for some adults to communicate, but for children the difficult task is compounded by not having fully developed expressive language skills. So actions (self-injury) can speak louder than words, and some children take advantage of this and experience it as successful.

❖ **Releasing the pain and tension the child feels** – a favorite activity for many adults to relieve stress is exercise. Consider what exercise actually does—it causes a different kind of pain (physical pain) rather than the mental strain of stress. It also helps with reducing tension by experiencing either a different type of tension or even a worse tension to relieve the original stress. In a similar way, some children find some relief from self-harm.

❖ **The illusion of control** – children frequently experience life as out of their control and this makes sense. Adults are in charge (or worse, no adults are in charge), they make the rules, they enforce the rules, and the child feels the only control is over his or her own body. Some children use bodily functions to express some level of control. A more serious type of perceived control is to harm oneself.

❖ **A distraction and temporary respite from the stress and pain of a problem existence** – one of the best interventions with young children is to distract them and refocus them from a problem behavior to a more desired behavior. Children also distract themselves. If you can't make the stress go away, try putting your focus elsewhere and see if you can make it at least take a background position for a time. Self-harm can be a powerful distractor.

❖ **Experiencing punishment that the individual believes is deserved** – children are quick to take a punitive stance with other children and with themselves. Much of this can come from their experience with adults who believe that punishment is the behavior modification of choice. More enlightened parenting has found that punishment, although it stops behavior in the short-term, actually increases the likelihood of the child punishing the adult or internalizing this orientation and believing he or she should be punished for all the problems.

❖ **Feeling anything other than numbness and dissociation** – although dissociation is an adaptation to overwhelming psychological pain, chronic dissociation produces a reaction in the brain that desires something other than the lack of sensation, and any stimulation will do. Therefore, the young person may prefer to feel badly than not feel anything at all.

All of these influences can result in the child's brain mistakenly believing that self-harm can be a good thing by being preferable to something worse. This type of thinking must be countered early in life if the child is to avoid habitual self-harming behavior. Self-harm is not a positive strategy to cope with the stress and pressure of living.

Jeffrey told us by his behavior how he was often treated in his home.

Jeffrey was seven and had been in foster care for three years. After this, he had been adopted into his current family. He was removed from his birth home due to physical abuse and neglect. When Jeffrey became frustrated, which was frequently, he often would hit himself in the face hard enough to cause nose bleeds. His records confirmed that this was one of the frequent experiences of physical abuse he received as a child, and it became a habitual pattern that needed to be changed. His treatment included: asking for support when feeling bad, putting more time into enjoyment and play, and reframing responsibility for his abuse in the home. With interventions designed for both his self-aggression and his frequent frustrations, his behavior improved significantly.

Prevention

Certainly the best way to prevent a serious problem like self-harm is to change the conditions that might cause it in the first place. Prevention can mean many things when it comes to self-harm. You could take action to reduce the conditions that could result in a young person wanting to harm him or herself (primary prevention). It might mean an intervention that addresses young people who have been identified as 'at risk' (secondary prevention). If there is already a problem, prevention could mean working to reduce the severity or frequency of the behavior (tertiary prevention). The best place to start is to instill in young people the ability to cope with the stress that can be very challenging as a young person.

Promoting Resiliency in Children

Resiliency is a concept that can help summarize what a child needs to take on a stressful world and successfully meet the inherent challenges. Resiliency basically means the ability to recover after a difficult experience or being able to bounce back following adversity. Resiliency is one of the most important traits of a successful person, and the foundations of resiliency begin early in childhood years. Raising a resilient child is perhaps the foremost method to prevent self-harm later on. There are a number of steps that are important to increase the resiliency of a child.

Basic needs must be met – for children who start life with the experience that the world responds to their many needs, the resulting internal working model is a positive and optimistic view of living. However, the opposite is true for children who cry out very early in life and find a hostile world where their needs are either ignored or inconsistently met. For these children the brain adapts to not expect help and support, and the result is a very young child who cannot rely on adults. But the child knows an adult is needed for basic needs to be met, and without assistance stress becomes chronic and toxic. The result is stress in massive amounts. Other results can include a lack of interest in attaching to adults, mood disorders such as depression, and other behavioral and mental health problems. When a child's basic needs are consistently met early in life, the result is a youngster who approaches situations in life with curiosity, openness and trust that adults will be there to provide support, and the child does not feel alone and frightened. This is the formula to instill resiliency in a child early in life.

Solid attachments at all ages – only when a child can rely on adults to meet basic needs will a child's brain be interested in reaching out and being vulnerable to parents or other adults. Attachments are the number one prescription for managing stress. When reaching out to an adult is consistently successful, the child's brain identifies bonding with an adult (or more than one adult) as the best way to survive and to thrive. When a child reaches out to an adult and finds inconsistent care and support, or finds none at all, the child's brain adapts and does not pursue bonds with others as an effective strategy. Since social attachments at every age of life are the key to stress reduction, attachments are a major prerequisite to resiliency and handling adversity.

Healthy internal working models – a child is unaware of what is and is not heathy; the only consideration of a child is who is going to protect me, care for me, provide for me, teach me and love me. The brain does not start life with judgments, it simply avoids what is harmful and pursues what is helpful to promote survival. The very early experience of a child will determine an orientation toward the environment, which includes people. When a child receives support to overcome obstacles, the result is a belief that difficulties can be overcome and opportunities exist to be able to try again after failure— this is resiliency training that can add to the child's internal working model of everyday life. Resilient children therefore have healthy (meaning positive and optimistic) internal working models of self, others and the world.

Social support to reduce stress – when basic needs are met and when healthy internal working models develop, there is the experience of bonding with others as an important method to overcome the many challenges of daily life. All these factors weave together to form a resilient child, or when absent, form an individual who struggles with anxiety, stress and fear. If this becomes chronic, the individual will likely struggle with depression and ultimately hopelessness.

Coping with the challenges of life – when children learn how to handle a difficult situation, this can be called coping with adversity. Coping is certainly related to resilience and is an excellent answer to the stress of life. Coping involves ample quantities of: social support, anticipating the challenge in advance (so it is not a surprise), having an outlet for your energy, feeling a sense of control, and optimistic attitude (Sapolsky, 2004). Individuals who are able to cope with living, particularly the difficult challenges of living, are not candidates to develop overwhelming anxiety, depression and hopelessness. Therefore, children (and adults) who learn to cope with stress seldom if ever engage in self-harm, so learning coping strategies can prevent NSSI.

Spot the Problem Early to Prevent Self-Harm

Due to the habitual nature of human behavior, catching self-harm early is critically important to addressing the problem. Some will argue that getting to a problem early before it becomes a more serious issue, or what is commonly called tertiary prevention, is not prevention at all. But this is an academic argument and does not change the fact that the earlier a pattern of self-harm can be addressed, the better for everyone.

All NSSI does not look the same — with some children wanting to be noticed and others hiding the injuries. Early detection is therefore much easier with some children than others. For the children and teens who hide this behavior, the first step is to spot the problem as soon as possible. There are a number of warning signs that can help an adult be more aware of self-harm.

- Physical injuries such as cuts and burns that seem unusual or have no clear cause. Look for such injuries on extremities.
- Being sensitive and reactive to questions from adults about an injury, such as a cut or burn.
- Be aware of unexplained signs of blood in a child's room.

- Frequent absence from others in the family or from friends and preferring to be alone often.
- Questionable explanations for behavior that caused harm in order to make it sound unintentional, such as "I was not paying attention" or "I don't remember how I fell."
- Finding unusual items the young person has that could cause self-injury, such as knives or even broken glass.
- Concealing marks on the skin by wearing clothes that hide the arms and legs.
- General depressed mood combined with any of the other warning signs.

When an adult does suspect a problem of self-harm, the tendency is to emotionally react, which is entirely understandable. No adult wants to learn that a child is intentionally being hurtful. However, a strong reaction when learning of the problem can damage the adult's ability to connect and be helpful to the young person. Children who hide self-harm do so because they anticipate disapproval and negative judgment from adults. Telling a child to stop doing the behavior, which is the understandable tendency most adults would have, could do more harm than good. The general rule when self-harm is either suspected or actually confirmed is to support the child, not judge or punish. The young person does not need either judgment or punishment from you, since he or she is already doing so internally. What the child needs is to feel the support from some source to reduce the anxiety and stress of everyday life, to not feel alone, and instead feel less hopeless because there is help available. A reactive parent, as understandable as this is, will generally make the situation worse, drive the behavior further underground, and increase the stress that caused the problem in the first place.

If a strong emotional response from the adult is not the answer, then what is the answer? Clearly, most adults will react strongly when learning of self-harm with a child. Pretending not to be upset by this is not effective. Adults should express what they feel and think—but not to the child. Self-harm not only hurts the involved child, it also impacts the adult, and everyone needs support. It is a good idea for the adult in this situation to get some personal support first before turning their attention to the child. This can be with a spouse, friend, pastor and, if such a person is not available, seek support from a professional therapist or counselor. The adult will be in no position to reduce the stress of the child until personal stress is reduced first.

Once the adult is thinking clearly and ready to address the problem in a calm and centered fashion, the goal of any intervention becomes some method to reduce the causes of the problem within the child—which are usually stress and anxiety.

Methods That Can Prevent Self-Harm

There are many organizations that can provide help and ideas regarding self-harm. One of these comes from the United Kingdom called Mind.org.uk. This organization identifies a number of strategies that adults and older teens can use to prevent self-harm even after it has become a negative habit. Some of the ideas will be too advanced for younger children, but some can help adults to help a child. Because the objective of self-harm can vary, so can the strategies. Here are a few from the mind.org.uk organization:

Instead of harming yourself in order to release strong emotions, here are some other steps an individual can take:

- Paint, draw, or scribble on a big piece of paper with red ink or paint
- Express feelings in a journal
- Compose a poem or song to express feelings
- Write down any negative feelings and then rip the paper up
- Listen to music that expresses what feelings come up

For younger children, the above could be suggested in an age appropriate way, particularly if the adult does the activities with the child and guides the child.

If the goal is to reduce stress and self-soothe, the following are offered:

- Take a bath or hot shower
- Pet or cuddle with a dog or cat
- Wrap up in a warm blanket
- Massage the neck, hands, and feet
- Listen to calming music

Once again, an adult could do any of the above with a child to give the child extra attention and support, while teaching the child coping skills to self-soothe.

When counteracting self-harm is intended to help the individual move from dissociated states and feelings to being more in the present, here are some ideas:

- Call a friend
- Take an invigorating shower
- Hold an ice cube in the crook of your arm or leg
- Chew something with a very strong taste, like chili peppers, peppermint, or a grapefruit peel
- Go online to a self-help website, chat room, or message board

If the objective is tension reduction or to express anger:

- Exercise vigorously—run, dance, jump rope, or hit a punching bag
- Punch a cushion or mattress, or scream into your pillow
- Squeeze a stress ball or squish Play-Doh or clay
- Rip something up (sheets of paper, a magazine)
- Make some noise (play an instrument, bang on pots and pans)
- Use a red felt tip pen to mark where you might usually harm yourself
- Rub ice across your skin rather than harm the skin
- Put rubber bands on wrists or arms and snap them rather than self-harming

All of these ideas are based on the individual wanting to reduce or prevent self-harm. To help the child, the contact with a supportive adult doing some of these activities may address the child's need to have the pain acknowledged, and the very act of engaging with the child may fulfill the need for support.

The following are for older teens who have a sincere interest in reducing self-harming behavior:

- Talk to someone – if you are on your own, perhaps you could phone a friend or call a hotline
- Do a favorite activity or hobby to change focus
- If the person you are with is making you feel worse, do something else
- Watch a favorite movie, particularly a comedy or one that lifts your spirits
- Distract yourself by going out, listening to music, or by doing something harmless that interests you

- Relax and focus your mind on something pleasant – your very own personal comforting place
- Find another way to express your feelings, such as squeezing ice cubes (which you can make with red juice to mimic blood if the sight of blood is important), or just drawing red lines on your skin
- Give yourself some 'harmless pain' - eat a hot chili, or have a cold shower
- Focus your mind on positive things
- Be kind to yourself – allow yourself to do something harmless that you enjoy
- Write a diary or a letter to explain what is happening to you – no one else needs to see it

[Much of the above was taken from mind.org.uk where more information and strategies can be found.]

Interventions for Non-Suicidal Self Injury

The most important part of the discussion is how to assist a young person to stop behavior that is harmful. The dynamics of self-harming behavior of all kinds is very complex, the behaviors are many and varied because the causes are complicated and unique to the individual. Addressing self-harming behavior cannot be reduced to a simplistic formula, which is the reason so much has been covered before addressing interventions. However, a thorough understanding of this problem does point to some themes that need to be a part of the solution.

As complex as self-harming behavior is, any attempt to prevent or decrease the severity and frequency will need to address these factors:

✓ Reduce the amount of stress the young person is feeling.

✓ Enhance coping skills to handle stress that can't be reduced.

✓ Listen and give the child a voice so he or she need not speak through problem behavior.

✓ Improve the young person's sense of confidence and self-esteem.

✓ Encourage connection and attachment with others to build social support.

✓ Find a substitute positive coping behavior for every self-harming behavior to be eliminated.

To help remember these important components, just recall the word RELIEF. With the above list as a guide, the complex aspects of self-harming behavior can be addressed by interventions that are individualized for the young person's unique situation. Although complicated, when interventions are individualized and address the above list, the solutions may be straightforward.

> Some very complex problems can have straightforward solutions.
>
> Over the years in the Jasper Mountain intensive residential treatment program, thousands of children have gone through the program, often with extreme problems. Among the problems have been hundreds of children with some type of an eating disorder (one type of self-harm)—too much, too little, eating non-edible substances, and more. Although the program has no specific eating disorder therapy, it does create an environment where stress is reduced, coping skills are taught, social support is provided, and new perceptions take the place of negative beliefs. The result is we are still waiting for the first child to come into the program with an eating disorder and leave with that same problem. These treatment elements can create an environment that naturally solves complex issues.

Dave Ziegler

Before putting the focus on the child, we will first focus on the adult who is trying to be of help. Facing self-harm with a child can be very difficult for any adult and can produce a host of reactions and emotions. In fact, the stress experienced by the young person can be deflected to the adult, who may struggle with the resulting stress. In an emotionally charged situation, it is important to remember that the adult must model what the goal is for the child. If the young person simply picks up the pressure, stress and urgency from the adult, all of which are understandable, the result may be more anxiety and making the situation worse rather than better. The message the helping adult wants the young person to receive is there are solutions to problems, and there are better ways to handle stress than to harm oneself. To effectively give this message, the adult must have a balance of thoughtfully connecting with the young person in a caring and sensitive manner. Too much or too little emotion and the results may backfire. The overall theme is to demonstrate to the child how to face a difficult situation, because, in fact, this is likely a very difficult situation for the adult. Here are some suggestions for the helper:

- Turn negative feelings about the behavior into supportive and caring feelings for the child. It is to be expected that, knowing a child or teen is intentionally self-harming, most any adult will be upset, angry, confused or even feel responsible. After all, isn't the adult supposed to ensure the safety of the child? To be supportive may require the adult to express strong negative feelings in some manner, but not in the presence of the young person and certainly not directed at the child.
- Be careful how you use information learned from the child. If the young person is honest about self-harm and receives disapproval and judgmental energy in return, the behavior may become much more covert.

96

The more the adult understands the real problem, rather than the observable symptoms, the more prepared, thoughtful, and helpful the response can be.

- Be available rather than distant. Upset emotional reactions can push a child away, and the child's stress can actually increase rather than decrease.

Because self-harm is a form of internalized aggression, the first goal is to take the behavior out of the shadows and have open communication with a supportive adult. The adult who wants to be helpful may need to hear some upsetting and difficult information, and unless this can be handled calmly, it may be the end of communication with the young person. You can't help if you don't know what is going on, and you can't come up with solutions unless you have a good understanding of the problem.

What Children Need and Don't Need from Parents and Helping Adults

Children who have chosen self-harm most often need the help of a rescuing adult. Self-harm is an unpleasant solution to overwhelming stress, but it may be the only solution the child can identify. Adults need to be there for the child—avoiding making the tension and stress worse and offering a steady hand to hold. There are a number of displayed characteristics that can be helpful. Adults are most helpful to troubled children when they demonstrate the following:

- ✓ Safe – there are different levels of safety, including physical as well as emotional safety. A young person may not disclose self-harm if they fear condemnation or not feeling emotionally safe. You will not be able to provide what the young person needs from you unless you are safe, as well as being perceived as safe.

✓ Consistent – when a child is in an internal or external crisis, what is needed is an adult who can handle the situation with a steady, consistent plan to make things better. The last thing a child needs is for the adult to crumble, become erratic and go into a personal crisis.

✓ Available – social support has already been identified as the best prescription for stress. Some adults faced with self-harm with a young person consciously or subconsciously create distance with the child. You cannot support a child unless you are present and available.

✓ Clear – it is common for young people under significant personal stress to have disorganized thoughts, feelings and behaviors. The reasoning centers of the brain are impacted by intense stress and internal conflicts. To help the young person think clearly you must model what this looks like.

✓ Unruffled – many confused children test adults while actually hoping the adult will pass the test. Self-harming children may become dramatic and, at times, seem out of control. What the child needs from the adult is a solid, determined and composed energy to counter erratic energy.

✓ Firm – support can take many forms, and at times it needs to come in the form of firm structure. It is a general rule that structure helps children feel more internally secure. Being firm can help, but how firmness is presented is important. Avoid authoritarian directives to stop problem behavior. Instead, institute predictable structure and provide a supportive firmness.

✓ Smart – when a child is in crisis or is confused, the reasoning centers of the child's brain take a back seat to the fear center of the brain, and the result can be chaos and more stress. The adult must maintain equilibrium and the ability to think clearly. The adult can bring the experience of overcoming difficult situations and thinking through the problem to come up with some solutions. A child must rely on a smart and resourceful adult for help.

✓ Confident – you may not know exactly what to do to help a young person with self-harming behavior, but this is not required to communicate an important level of confidence. You must be confident that you will find workable answers and solutions, you must be confident that you will help the child to improve the situation. If you are not confident, then get help for yourself to become confident, otherwise you will offer less than what the child needs from you.

✓ Supportive – in everything you do to help, learn and reach out to the child, do so with a consistent attitude of being supportive. You may need to ignore some of what the young person says when he or she is testing you and demands to be left alone, for example. But learn to translate a cry for help even when the youngster's words say the opposite of what they really mean.

✓ Optimistic - depression comes, in part, from feelings of hopelessness. The best answer is optimism. Not only does the child need your optimism, you also need your optimism. The path to helping a young person with self-harm may take time, and there may be relapses and failures along the way. Being optimistic about long-term success is what everyone needs, particularly the young person.

> **Colleen put objects into her body**
>
> Young children, at times, put objects into orifices of the body, and this is common enough that it is not considered abnormal. However, the frequency and type of object can be a sign of early self-harm. As we worked with Colleen to stop putting objects into her vaginal and anal areas, the behavior decreased. However, one day she complained about pain on the left side of her head. When she was seen in urgent care, the doctor was surprised to find a plastic pearl from costume jewelry pushed deep within her ear. It was a challenge for the medical staff to remove it, and it was clear we had more work to do to help Colleen.

Take the above suggested personal traits and invest them into strategies that can be helpful with the problem of self-harm. Here are ten suggested strategies to consider. The age of the young person, the circumstances and the specific factors in each situation are unique, so consider how to use the following to develop a plan of action with Non-Suicidal Self-Injury:

1. Work to change the child's perceptions – Since behaviors are the outgrowth of perceptions and emotions, the best place to effect a change is at the beginning with perceptions. There are many perceptions of the young person that are behind self-harm—things are bad in my life and I have no ability to make things better, I am not strong enough to face the stress in my life, not only are things bad but they are getting worse, the only time anyone cares is when I upset them by hurting myself, and many more such perceptions. It is clear to the adults, but not to the young person that these perceptions are mostly false. When a child is not thinking clearly, he or she needs a supportive adult to help think clearly. Change the

child's perceptions and it will change their experience and their behavior.

2. Disconfirm the negative model the young person believes – Part of changing perceptions is to counter the internal working model that drives how the child thinks and feels. The adult must identify the negative beliefs of the young person and work to change these beliefs by disconfirming them. Although this can sometimes be done in verbal ways, the best way to disconfirm is to have the child experience something at odds with the child's internal model. For example, the thought of not having any control can be disconfirmed by giving a child more control over some aspects of his or her life. The negative model of not being strong enough to handle stress can be disconfirmed by an adult commenting on how well a child handled a difficult situation.

3. Teach the child several forms of relaxation and model what you teach – Research has confirmed that teaching a troubled person forms of relaxation can be one of the most important strategies for any problem, but particularly for self-harm (Barnes, P.M., Bloom, B. & Nahin, R.L. 2008; Weisz, 2014). Self-harm has one of its primary causes from uncontrolled stress and the inability to manage the stress. Learning skills to cope with stress, such as various forms of relaxation, is a targeted intervention with a strong likelihood of improving the child's experience and self-efficacy.

4. Promote positive play and recreation – At every developmental age play is an important component of a healthy individual. Although this is true even for seniors, it is even more true for children. The term 'recreation' comes from re-creating ourselves through investing in something fun. The primary job of a child is to learn and to play. Many children with a traumatic history and children who self-harm have lost the

interest and sometimes even the ability to truly play — meaning to lose oneself in the joy of an activity that has no utilitarian purpose outside of the enjoyment. An important part of any intervention with these children should be the encouragement and participation with the child in enjoyable play (Ziegler, 2012).

5. Work to build the bond with the child; social support is the best stress reliever for children – The quality of a child's attachments with others, particularly primary care providers, may be the single most important element of good mental health. Without strong attachments, negative experiences impact the child's self-perceptions, confidence, relationships with others and, principally, the ability to cope with stress. Working to improve an attachment with a young person who is engaged in self-harming behavior can have positive results far beyond this one problem behavior and may improve overall mental health (Schore, 2001).

6. Translate the meaning of the self-harming behavior to the child – Understanding the behavior is critically important to develop effective interventions. Translating behavior is to consider the meaning of the behavior to the child. What is the child saying through the behavior? The answer may be very different than an adult may initially think. This approach has been found to be extremely effective in treatment interventions with some of the most damaged children (Ziegler, 2005). Finding the right translation takes experience and understanding the specific child. However, adults can practice this skill and learn quickly to apply intuition to the situation, come up with possible translations, consider what may be the most likely, and test the resulting premise. We will soon go through this process with a real case of self-harm in this section.

7. Develop strategies to match the emotional age of the young person – Response to substantial stress is a very effective indicator of the emotional development and maturity of a young person (and also an adult). Under stress the brain naturally becomes more reactive through the stress response cycle (explained in Part II). The limbic brain is a major player in how the brain processes emotions and traumatic memories. Stress is often mentally associated with the past, particularly the traumatic past. These factors help explain why an individual under stress reverts to his or her emotional age, which is often associated with the age the individual experienced trauma. Knowing this should help intervening at the individual's emotional age for better outcomes.

8. Provide executive functions from outside the child's brain – Research on brain development has pointed out the reality that experiences not only impact the brain, they form the architecture of the brain. Taking this one step further, if a traumatized child is primarily reacting to events, the brain will strengthen the reactive responses. However, if an adult sees that the child is not using higher order reasoning and consideration, then the adult can assist the child in the areas lacking, which will generally be the many executive functions of the pre-frontal cortex. Therefore, when an adult assists the young person to: calmly think about the situation, relax, consider possible options to respond, consider the ramifications of the response based upon past experience, etc., the child's brain actually changes over time with help from the outside. This means that any adult with the right approach can impact positive brain changes that include the section of the brain the child uses most often, as well as actual physical changes in neuro-template development.

9. Know the right problem before trying to solve it – The principle has been already addressed that to be effective with your interventions requires that you can distinguish between symptoms and the core problem. An adult need not be an expert in self-harm behavior and interventions; the adult simply needs to be an expert in this one child and what is going on within the child's perceptions and emotions. When 'nothing seems to work' it may be that what you are doing is addressing the wrong topic.

10. The immediate issue is important, but remember to take a long-term perspective – One of the most frequent weakness of adults helping young people is they get in a hurry, restrict their focus, and consider only what needs to be done right here and right now. While this is important when a child is engaging in self-injurious behavior, it is not the only important consideration. To be most helpful, adults need to take a long-term view of what the child will need tomorrow, next week, a year from now and later in life. Build problem-solving skills rather than always telling the child what to do, teach a child to reduce internal stress and not just how to avoid the stress. When a short-term and a long-term perspective are considered, it is the latter that can have the best outcomes.

Two case studies will now be presented to show a process of developing a response to self-harming behavior that can provide a good probability of success. This approach will continue with the theme that to be helpful you do not need to be an expert in self-harming behavior; you just need to be an expert on the young person you are trying to help. Therefore, this process will provide important steps to understand the behavior, understand the child, and combine these to overcome the problem. This process is referred to as the

Neurological Reparative Therapy Intervention Protocol (see Appendix).

Neurological Reparative Therapy

Don't be put off by the complicated sounding name, this approach is helping young people with histories of trauma heal based on their personal potential. It is an approach anyone can use and it is just what the name says: the goal is to promote positive brain change (neurological); it begins with healing past trauma and returning the brain to its normal state of seeking to thrive (repair) and it is an active process (therapy which anyone can implement) of intervening to achieve the five goals: 1. help change the child's perceptions of self, others and the world, 2. enhance the brain's cohesion to have all parts of the brain work together, or neuro-integration, 3. alter the part of the brain that makes decisions, 4. encourage development of the part of the brain that uses higher reasoning—the orbitofrontal cortex, and 5. build new brain pathways and strengthen these through repetitive practice. More information is available on this approach to make lasting change (Ziegler, 2011).

Case Study #1 – Donald's Active Self-Harm

Donald was seven years old when he was referred for mental health care. Self-harm was only one of the many problem behaviors exhibited by this disturbed young man. His history read like many young people who develop self-harm, but it was much more serious than most. His biological mother had a problem with drugs and alcohol, but either she was not using during pregnancy, or the impact of substance abuse was not a primary part of Donald's developmental profile. However, serious neglect and physical and sexual abuse were dominant factors from his earliest experience. The abuse was so bad that it can best be referred to as torture. The abuse was both terrible in method and chronic in its frequency. There were several protective services investigations when he reached school age (often the case with serious abuse due to no one outside the family knowing about the abuse until the child begins to get outside the home). Donald was initially left in the home and finally removed. By this time the chronic trauma had gone on for years, and this young child knew only a world where his needs were not attended to, and his body was used and abused by sadistic parents.

Due to the intensity of the abuse and length of time over which it occurred, Donald was diagnosed with a variety of serious psychological disorders, including dissociative disorders (lack of responsiveness and lack of being present) and delusional psychosis (having an alternative reality). With his other problems, Donald also frequently (multiple times per day) harmed himself. Donald was a child who had a combination of presentations that are typical for self-harming young people—instead of having one pattern, he had multiple patterns. He used overt and covert self-harm. He intentionally hurt himself with any method available, he did so in a way that he was familiar with, and he seemed to think he deserved the harm. He would cut, burn, tear his skin, bite himself, drink harmful substances and throw himself into walls. He often seemed to be punishing himself for some offense. He also appeared to harm himself as a way to feel something other than numbness. Each time he would hurt himself it seemed to be from a different motivation. Donald had a much more complex array of issues than most children who harm themselves, and his situation required the right setting (a psychiatric residential treatment program) and intensive assessments and interventions to help him heal and improve.

The first step in our process, to help understand and come up with potentially effective interventions for Donald, is to consider the meaning of the self-harming behavior to him. This can be done by translating the behavior.

Translating Donald's behavior – the wide range and frequency of the problem self-harming behavior can only be considered extreme. If Donald was not watched at all times, and even when he was watched, he would find ways to hurt himself very intentionally. As with other children with either many problem behaviors or very frequent serious issues, it is important not to be overwhelmed.It is best to begin with something specific rather than trying to do everything at once. This can be done by choosing a "target symptom." This term acknowledges that one behavior is chosen, but it is not the problem but a symptomatic outgrowth of a deeper problem. This can help improve the odds of effective interventions by identifying the correct problem that is causing the issues that are observable.

The beginning target symptom chosen was Donald biting himself to the point of breaking the skin and bleeding daily and in most settings. It was clear that this would be only one of many target symptoms that must be addressed to help Donald with his many problems. But if some success could be achieved in one specific area, this could make both the adults and the child feel some progress and relieve some stress. Because of Donald's serious history of trauma, the role of healing his past abuse would need to be an important element of helping him move forward.

Target Symptom – Donald bites himself causing some level of injury on a daily basis when he is upset, bored and sometimes for no known reason.

Translating the Behavior – our next step is to climb inside Donald's thinking and emotions to better understand the meaning of the behavior to him. This can be done by a process of considering multiple possible meanings, and then attempting to come up with a working hypothesis as to the meaning of the behavior to the child. It is understood that the hypothesis could be incorrect, but this will be discovered as the process unfolds. Here are some possible translations of Donald's target symptom:

- o Pain is all I am familiar with.
- o I hate myself and want to hurt my body.
- o I hurt myself out of habit.
- o I like the concern and attention I get from adults when I do something hurtful to myself.
- o I would rather feel pain than feel nothing.
- o I want to die.
- o The sight of blood tells me that I am real.
- o I cannot do anything about what is going on around me, but I can exercise control over myself by being hurtful.
- o I do bad things all the time, and I should be punished.
- o I have the voice of a demon in my head telling me to hurt myself.
- o If I hurt myself, then the adults may decide not to hurt me.
- o I can't tell if any part of my world is real.

It is suggested that the list of possible translations be at least 7 but not more than 12. This will encourage consideration of numerous possibilities. Adults frequently consider their first thought to be the best possibility, but this is seldom correct. A further suggestion to help 'think outside the box' is to list at least two unusual or bizarre translations. In this list above, the two unusual translations are the third to last and the last items. The next step is to narrow down the items to form a working hypothesis or best guess of what the child is saying by the behavior being displayed. To do this each item is reviewed, and it requires you to use your insight to come up with your first thought on whether this is not what the child is saying by the behavior (-), or has some element of the child's message (+), or appears to be exactly what is the most accurate statement (++).

- o + Pain is all I am familiar with – while this appears to be true, it does little to help with understanding or developing a response.
- o - I hate myself and want to hurt my body – adaptive behavior is not a sign of self-hate but more a sign of doing whatever possible to survive.
- o - I hurt myself out of habit – although there is an element of habitual behavior, of itself this does not seem to be the best translation.
- o - I like the concern and attention I get from adults when I do something hurtful to myself – attention is often one aspect of self-harming behavior in that it is reaching out to be rescued. In Donald's case, he does not consider rescue to be available and is not motivated by attention.
- o ++ I would rather feel pain than feel nothing – his pattern of dissociation and having a vacant affect makes this translation appear to be on target.
- o - I want to die – this does not fit for a child who has lived for years with constant abuse and has continued to struggle to survive.
- o ++ The sight of blood tells me that I am real – Donald has difficulty differentiating between his delusional world and objective reality. Pain and blood appear to ground him in the present based on the strength of the physical and visual sensations.
- o + I cannot do anything about what is going on around me, but I can exercise control over myself by being hurtful – this appears to be accurate, but more of a secondary motivation.
- o + I do bad things all the time and I should be punished – his negative sense of self fits his view of being bad, but this does not appear to be a primary factor.

- ○ ++ I have the voice of a demon in my head telling me to hurt myself – although this may seem a strange translation, it turns out that Donald does hear the voices of his abusive parents due to the traumatic memories he has, and the demon in this case is the legacy of his sadistic biological parents.
- ○ - If I hurt myself, then the adults may decide not to hurt me – this is the case with some children when they harm themselves, but does not fit well with Donald.
- ○ ++ I can't tell if any part of my world is real – once again this translation meant to be unusual turns out to be endorsed as a major factor for Donald. Self-harm and the resulting sensations help him tell fantasy from reality, and in this way the self-harm is experienced as a positive behavior to him.

Considering each of the above, the result was five items that seemed to be off base or not the best translations. There were two items that were on target, but only partially accurate. There were four items that were considered in the process to be the best translations. Notice that two of them were the unusual or bizarre items; this often happens when using this process. The next step is to combine the items that were endorsed to come up with a working translation of what the child is telling us. In this case the four items could be combined to say something like—"I don't know what is real and what isn't because of the voices inside and outside of me; I hurt myself to find what is real." This translation fits this child's delusional and dissociative diagnoses and will be taken into the next step of the process.

Does the child speak in opposites? A frequent dynamic with a seriously traumatized child is a pattern of using language to communicate the opposite of what the young person is actually saying. Many adults get stuck on a child's words, and this is often a mistake. To consider whether this child is speaking in opposites, it is helpful to write down frequent statements the child makes and then write down the opposite and see which is more accurately what the child is communicating.

For Donald here are some of his verbal statements:

Statement/Opposite

> - I am fine, leave me alone/I am lost please help me.
> - I won't follow your rules/I need structure, it is comforting.
> - I don't need anything from anyone/Without your help I am in trouble.
> - I am a crazy person/Help me not be crazy.
> - I like to hurt myself/I don't know what else to do.
> - Life is hopeless/Help me find some hope.

Some traumatized young people go back and forth with their statements; sometimes they say what they mean but often they speak in opposites. In the examples above, the opposite meaning of Donald's frequent statements in each case appeared to be what he was really attempting to communicate.

Our next step is to consider the potential causes when a child struggles with what is real and what is not real, and uses self-harm to help feel some level of being grounded in reality. To consider causes, it is helpful to review the child's past and ask the question 'what could produce a child who thinks, feels and acts this way?' Recall from the initial comments about Donald that he had years of terrible abuse (no specifics will be given here, but the adults were harmful in intentional and sadistic ways). Donald's brain did not know what a healthy child should experience from parents; all he knew was pain and abuse. To adapt to the situation at hand, his brain created an alternative world where there was less suffering. To psychiatrists, this healthy adaptation was a mental health problem of delusional and dissociative states. This alternative world was a healthy adaptation to a very unhealthy environment, but in a supportive environment it was not a healthy adaptation. However, when children are traumatized early, and the most frequent age of trauma is below age 1, they only know the reality they have. In Donald's case he could not manage or cope with the environment he found himself in, and his brain created one to help him survive. When he was removed from the traumatic environment, his adaptations moved into the unhealthy realm. But it is quite clear when developing our working translation of the self-harm behavior that this could be a direct consequence of the background information on Donald's early developmental history and the terrible amount of trauma he experienced.

The next step is to develop interventions to address the target symptom of Donald biting himself to experience the pain and resulting bleeding. This may seem like a slow and cumbersome process at first, but consider what is now clear about the situation with Donald that would not have been evident if the response to his self-harm would have been an upset adult doing the first intervention that came to mind to just make the self-harm stop. With this process the focus is not only on the short-term symptom behavior, but also long-term needs of the child. We will now move to the intervention stage armed with all the information we have pulled together.

It is helpful to consider a list of interventions without evaluating them until after the list is developed. Also consider the components of effective interventions in the mnemonic aid RELIEF mentioned previously—thus keeping in mind the translations (climbing inside the world of the young person to understand the meaning of the behavior), while considering the past experiences that could result in the observable behavior. Now comes the important step of considering possible interventions.

1. Change the grounding in reality from blood and pain to interpersonal connection with others.
2. Have an adult prepared to spot stressful situations and lend immediate assistance to help lower the stress by teaching coping skills.
3. Set aside time each day for some brief, quality interactions with a trusted adult (parent, teacher, or mentor).
4. Encourage daily play and fun in whatever the young person is interested in; most anything is more positive than self-harm, even video games (generally video games are not recommended for children with reality issues, but distraction and enjoyment in Donald's takes precedence).
5. Work to have Donald experience safety in his environment through structure and consistency, with all basic needs being unconditionally met.
6. Allow an interest in positive fantasy, but point out how it is different from reality.
7. Point out the times Donald handles stressful situations well to improve his sense of self-confidence.
8. Provide a mentor for Donald who has no parental or authority role of making rules. The focus is on relationship building, attachment skills, and having fun together.
9. Consider if the level of Donald's stress is significant enough for medication to aid in reducing it to a level he can take steps to manage it further. This would involve a consult with a child psychiatrist.
10. Increase the amount of supervision Donald has so an adult can be more aware of his stress level and any signs that self-harming behavior may take place. It is often best to supervise closely without being obvious or

the child may become more covert and the behavior become secretive.

There are many more interventions that could be identified, but the goal is not to have as many as possible. The goal is to come up with a manageable number of approaches that may have the best chance at reducing the problem behavior. It is not a good idea to implement all or even many interventions at once. Your energy and attention can become divided and scattered, and you may not recognize what is helping and what is not helping. A suggestion is start with three to five interventions and prepare to adjust, add or subtract based upon evaluating what seems to be helping.

The very first thing that may help the adult is to have a positive plan of action. This generally reduces the amount of stress the adult has because something specific is being done about the issue. The next thing that may help is the child picks up the improved energy from the adult and may feel more hopeful and less hopeless about the perceived overwhelming parts of his or her life.

In Donald's case the initial focus became two main issues — safety and stress reduction through social support. To accomplish the goals, intervention 5 was the first target, and all aspects of Donald's day were considered for how clear, predictable structure could lower his stress. This included very specific things like having a firm bedtime each night, having dinner at a regular hour, having an evening structure after dinner that included time with adults and stress relieving and enjoyable activities. Structure is often the first step to improving a child's sense of safety.

The next focus went to social support as a means to lower stress. In Donald's case we were able to combine a number of the proposed interventions such a 1 - 4 - 8 to increase the time he had with caring, supportive adults. This left him alone less often, increased the presence of an adult (with more supervision) and gave Donald the sense of connection.

The last step in the process is to evaluate the results of the interventions and make adjustments as needed. It is usually helpful to have a benchmark of how often a problem behavior is taking place before starting an intervention. A common mistake by adults is to gauge success on only one factor—the total elimination of the problem behavior. Self-harming behavior is one of the problem behaviors among young people that may need to gradually improve and not disappear all at once. Therefore, it is helpful to know if the behavior is increasing or decreasing in severity and frequency.

Another mistake adults often make is to try something and get frustrated if the improvement is not instantaneous. Many behaviors may actually get worse initially, even with the right intervention. Essentially, no intervention is immediately and permanently effective and, therefore, it should be expected that changes and adjustments will be needed over time. Begin evaluating specific interventions after 30 days, it may take that long to move beyond the initial escalation stage (where behavior gets worse before getting better).

When considering how effective the interventions are, one measuring stick is to once again use the RELIEF factors to see if the child is reflecting improvement in each of the areas of stress reduction, more connectedness with others, and more interest in enjoyable activities, among other points. There are situations where an intervention could reduce the target symptom only to have another problem behavior develop or increase, and the overall situation is actually worse. Make sure to take time to evaluate the impact of your interventions (a step often overlooked by many adults), and expect to make changes and adjustments rather than feel disappointed when the first step proved less effective than hoped.

The examples in this book of children and behaviors are actual cases, as is Donald's. With this case the results of the interventions took time and required many adjustments. There were some immediate positive improvements, but other issues took persistence and patience. The end result was that Donald was able to improve not only with eliminating self-harm entirely, but he did not meet the clinical criteria for any mental health disorder at discharge from the program. In formal follow ups at 6, 12, 36, and 60 months, his improvement not only maintained but was better over time. In Donald's situation, it was clear he had no interest in hurting himself once he experienced a different and supportive world that did not put him at risk for abuse from others.

Case Study #2 – Jessica's Passive Self-Harm

Twelve-year-old Jessica fit the behavior pattern of many young girls who have experienced trauma due to physical and sexual abuse. In her case, her mother had a series of men coming into the family with none of them staying for any period of time. Jessica never met her biological father, and two of her mother's boyfriends were physically and sexually abusive to Jessica. Her mother was like many single mothers, she was simply trying to survive. She had trouble supporting and caring for herself and had little energy left over for Jessica. She therefore would leave Jessica under the supervision of a boyfriend simply to do things like get groceries or go to appointments with her Vocational Rehabilitation caseworker. At these times, she learned later, that one of the men sexually molested Jessica and the other had poor boundaries, exposing Jessica to sexually explicit material. Finding out that her daughter was sexually abused by individuals she trusted did not make her feel better about herself as a person or mother.

Jessica had an internalizing response to the abuse; she kept her pain and her feelings inside. She did not tell her mother about the abuse — in part not wanting to have her mother get angry and stop loving her. She therefore sought no rescue and kept her secret to herself. Keeping silent was not a healthy strategy since she began to hurt herself in ways that were not obvious to anyone, particularly her mother. This pattern of internalizing her pain is more often a female and very young child response, while boys will often externalize problem behaviors. For Jessica the only time an adult, usually her caring and sensitive teacher, noticed a problem was to see the signs of self-harm that were often hidden and subtle. Jessica's self-harming behavior included: eating very little while pretending to eat more than she did, she would pick at her skin and had numerous sores, usually on areas of her body that did not show, and her stress level also was evidenced by her pulling out her hair while in bed at night. Often the only visible symptom of her pain was her depression and lack of interest in playing and enjoying herself.

Unfortunately, Jessica's internalized reaction to her traumatic abuse went on for years. She was finally referred for intensive mental health care when it was discovered that her depression and self-harm were probably linked to the newly discovered sexual abuse she experienced. At that point, Jessica entered our psychiatric residential treatment program. Her initial presentation was of a twelve-year-old who was many years younger than her chronological age. She was very small for her age and had a very shy demeanor. She had a hollow, but ever present smile that was designed to hide what she was actually feeling. Jessica fit the pattern of a young person who harmed herself but did not want others to know. When it comes to treating externalizing and internalizing individuals, it is the latter that present a more difficult and complex challenge.

Following the Neurological Reparative Therapy Intervention Protocol provided in the Appendix, step one is to identify the target symptom that will be the focus of interventions. This does not necessarily mean identifying the most serious problem behavior, but the chosen behavior that will be the first target of interventions. At times it is not advisable to start with the most complex or serious issue, but rather to build toward very difficult behaviors by starting with a more manageable issue. At other times it is imperative, due to safety concerns for the young person, to move right to the most serious issue. Jessica had multiple problem areas, including her depressed mood, her affect that lacked authenticity, and her covert self-harm. We will focus here on her specific pattern of self-harm. So the target symptom (we view the target issue as a symptom rather than the deeper problem) is Jessica hurts herself almost daily in a variety of ways and does her best to hide this behavior from others.

We next want to translate her self-harming behavior by attempting to go inside her thinking and her emotions to come up with what she is saying through the behavior. Following the Protocol, at least ten to twelve possible translations will be identified.

- o I hate myself and I take my anger out in ways to be hurtful.
- o I am very confused and I hurt myself without even thinking about it.
- o I am filled with bad feelings, please rescue me from myself.
- o Feeling pain is a distraction from being depressed or feeling nothing at all.

- o I hurt myself when I get bored and don't have anything else to do.
- o I like the control I feel when hurting myself because I am in charge.
- o If I make myself unattractive, then I won't be sexually abused again.
- o I really want to die, but I don't know how to kill myself yet.
- o When I hurt myself I don't think all my bad thoughts.
- o I have another personality inside me who does the hurting.
- o It is really my Mom's boyfriend who makes me hurt myself.

We cannot know for sure just what the young person is saying through the behavior, but it can help to consider a number of possibilities. Once again there were two unusual translations listed to help consider 'outside the box' statements. As we did in Case Study #1, someone who best knows the young person goes over the list of potential translations and puts a (-) when it least fits, a (+) when the statement is true but not the best translation, and (++) when the translation is believed to be most on target.

- o - I hate myself and I take my anger out in ways to be hurtful – although this could be true for some young people, in Jessica's case neither the anger nor the intentionality fit well.
- o + I am very confused and hurt myself without even thinking about it – the confusion fits well, but she is more aware of her actions than to consider her hurting herself in a dissociative state.
- o - I am filled with bad feelings, please rescue me from myself – the fact that Jessica works so hard not to have the self-harm noticed does not seem to indicate that she uses the behavior to cry out for help.

- + Feeling pain is a distraction from feeling depressed or feeling nothing – this item fits but seems to be more thoughtful than Jessica presents.
- − I hurt myself when I get bored and don't have anything else to do – her self-harm does not appear to be a hobby or pastime; it appears to have a more insidious motive.
- − I like the control I feel when hurting myself because I am in charge – most traumatized children have an explicit interest in having control over their surroundings. However, Jessica expresses very little energy in this direction.
- + If I make myself unattractive, then I won't be sexually abused again – this motivation can be correct for many sexually abused young girls. This translation fits in Jessica's case, although she does not exhibit fearful energy or present concern for being sexually abused in the environment she is in.
- − I really want to die, but I don't know how to kill myself yet – Jessica does not appear to want to end her life, and her self-harm lacks an intent that is serious.
- ++ When I hurt myself I don't think all my bad thoughts – this item fits in a particular way since Jessica does obsess with bad thoughts. Self-harm could in fact be a very potent distraction from what bothers her the most—her negative thoughts.
- − I have another personality inside me who does the hurting – once again this item could fit for many traumatized children, but is not a good fit for Jessica whose behavior may be troubled, but it is consistently troubled.
- ++ It is really my Mom's boyfriend who makes me hurt myself – this item seems to have particular validity because Jessica relives her sexual abuse repeatedly. In a real way she may be experiencing a dark presence of a

past abuser that now may be herself, but her internal experience may be the abuser is inside of her.

Unlike our first case study with Donald, most of the translations did not fit well for Jessica. In a way, this points to how challenging it is to genuinely understand young people who internalize and hide their pain and self-harm. All of the possible translations could easily fit for another child with a problem with self-harm, but Jessica is somewhat more difficult to understand. Three of the possible translations did fit but were not highly endorsed. That left two items that form the working translation of Jessica's self-harming behavior. As was true with Donald, one of the unusual items best fit the perception of Jessica's message. The two translations that were most endorsed had to do with her perseverative negative thoughts.

Jessica's mood problems and her depression, in particular, appear to arise from her thoughts of past trauma and how little personal value she sees in herself. The distraction of the sensations of self-harm may be functional for a young girl who would rather feel pain than think chronic negative thoughts. She may experience the former sexual abuser still in her life (through her thoughts and traumatic memory), and this is indicated by her hurting herself silently in her bed at night and, at times, even during her sleep states. Therefore, the working theory of translating Jessica's self-harming behavior is her negative thoughts are the primary problem, both waking and sleeping, and she seeks some relief through pain and harming herself.

The protocol step involving consideration of whether Jessica talks in opposites is more helpful with externalizing children. This step can be helpful to look beyond a young person's verbal statements. However, for Jessica and other internalizing children, this step may not be informative or necessary.

Our next step is to ask what in the child's experience might produce the target issue that we have chosen to focus on. In Jessica's case, the magnitude of the sexual abuse she experienced at a young age, along with the fact that more than one perpetrator was involved, is our first cause to consider. In many ways, when a young child encounters sexual abuse, it essentially involves all the many types of other abuse — neglect, physical harm, and emotional harm. This can easily be understood and does not require a detailed explanation. But perhaps the two most critical impacts of sexual abuse involve the lack of a sense of safety, which is a serious aspect of neglect, and a loss of personal worth. Neglect is the type of childhood abuse with the most pervasive and long-term impacts. When a child does not experience safety and predictably getting all basic needs met, the child's internal working model is that constant vigilance (toxic stress) is required because at any moment things could go terribly wrong. The second impact is the child has an experience of being the prey and seeing adults as predators. If this internal perception in childhood is not altered by experience and healing, the mental frameworks of this negative model solidify over time rather than get better.

In Jessica's case, these two impacts of childhood sexual abuse appear to fit. First, she did not experience the safety she needed to avoid being the object of an adult's sexual gratification. This was combined with her feeling she was the target of a predator. This victimization would most often produce anxiety and stress that may result in dissociative adaptations such as delusional thinking, developing a private world in which she would not include others, and having an external presentation while having an internal realm that others were not allowed to enter. Within this inner world, her negative thoughts about the past and her fear of the present and future produced a coping style based on self-harm. When adults climb into Jessica's inner world, it only makes sense why this young person would have developed the behaviors that otherwise seem bizarre and illogical. Armed with our working translation and doing our best to understand what in Jessica's past has created the problem behavior, we have now built a foundation upon which we can attempt interventions that address the deeper problem, not just the symptom behavior.

Interventions – when the above process is followed, what may seem time consuming initially (it does not take much time with practice) can help a great deal when the goal is an effective response with interventions targeting the deeper problem. The primary goal is to help Jessica become more external and expressive. Be aware this may be one of those situations that initially may seem like the problem has increased. If the effort to externalize her pain is successful, than the overt self-harm may in fact increase in the short-term. But it is the external expression of pain that gives healing a much better chance in the long-term. The other perception that the target symptom has increased may come from the behavior going from covert to overt, and the frequency and severity of self-harm may be greater than was known. With these factors in mind, here are possible interventions in no particular order:

1. Encourage engagement in social activities – group activities with peers her age would be recommended, and the more active the better. It is probable that Jessica has difficulty being able to play and enjoy herself. Some children must be specifically taught to have fun after serious traumatic experiences.
2. Give Jessica a colorful rubber band to wear on her wrist that she can snap whenever she needs a distraction

from negative thoughts – this sounds like a gimmick, but it has helped many individuals become more aware, and it replaces one self-harming sensation with another less serious one.

3. Pursue professional trauma therapy that may include a group for young sexually abused females - sexual abuse is a form of trauma that can get worse rather than better over time, and it is best addressed with professional help. Healing should be the goal, and the presence of perseverative negative thoughts of abuse can be addressed by an experienced professional. Group therapy can be a very powerful component of professional help.

4. Give Jessica a red flag on a stick that she can place in a bottle whenever she is feeling particularly negative or has thoughts of self-harm – this is one of many ways that could be used to move toward externalizing covert thoughts and feelings. Initially praise her use of this approach rather than immediately have a serious discussion. The first step is to let her care provider know when things are difficult.

5. Find a weekly activity that both Jessica and her mother enjoy and something they can do together – this could involve any number of things: shopping, walking, dancing, playing a favorite game, seeing a movie, working in a garden, etc. The immediate message is her mother is tuning into Jessica rather than a past message that she felt unimportant to her mother.

6. If Jessica does not have a pet, animals can be potent components in the healing process – of course getting a pet can be a major project, but pets can be anything from a gold fish to a puppy. Make sure getting a pet is not an afterthought and everyone is ready for the responsibility. If so, a pet can be a wonderful way for a child to engage with her environment and get personal support back.

7. Work to minimize time Jessica is alone with her thoughts, at least initially – being alone initially is not what Jessica needs: she needs contact, active pursuits, and to externalize as much of her inner world as possible.

The goal is not quantity of interventions but quality of steps that may have a chance to improve the situation. Children who internalize their pain can be very challenging and may take patience. Several of the above potential interventions could be combined. Item 3 should receive immediate consideration, and if group therapy is involved this could address other items. Interventions 4 and 5 are steps that may also be effective. Item 2 could be done at any time, but it may be something to be included as a second step when more externalizing is occurring. While pets can be wonderful in the healing process, they also can be expensive, time consuming and depending on the type of pet, it can add to the stress of a household. So this intervention should be carefully considered beforehand.

Evaluation – the last step of this thoughtful process is to identify the outcome of the intervention. Perhaps the first question is 'How long do I continue the intervention before evaluating?' In a real sense, evaluation starts with the first time you implement your plan and continues throughout each step. However, there is a timeframe that can generally be used, and that period is a month. For a variety of reasons, an intervention may either start slowly or in some cases be immediately successful, but begin to fail soon after. Give the approach enough time to go through stages such as: initial stumbles, the child's potential reactivity, quick and easy success without staying power, etc. At the one month mark consider what seems to be working the best, what is clearly not working, and what adjustments might improve the outcome of what you are trying to do. When an intervention is discarded, it is a good time to go back to the initial list of potential interventions and move further down the list and try something else.

Considering the goal to bring RELIEF to the situation, each factor can be compared to our plan of assistance.

- ✓ Reduce the amount of stress – social support is the best way to address stress reduction, and the initial plan for Jessica increases social support.
- ✓ Enhance coping skills - although it is a simplistic step, item 2 gives Jessica both a plan and control over the process and is a form of coping.
- ✓ Listen and give the child a voice - item 4 gives Jessica a voice in a non-verbal way to express herself. Item 6 involves Jessica in deciding what activities to do and her opinion is important.
- ✓ Improve the young person's sense of confidence and self-esteem – perhaps the most useful item for this goal of improving is item 3 that must improve her self-confidence to be successful.
- ✓ Encourage attachment – attachment is addressed in items 3, 4 and 5.
- ✓ Find a substitute positive coping behavior – initially item 2 is a quick and easy way to provide an alternative behavior, and item 3 should be able to provide additional behaviors over time.

Reviewing the RELIEF items assures that we have addressed each of the goals to give the intervention plan a solid basis to be successful. As the plan is adjusted and items are added and subtracted, the RELIEF items can be of help to guide changes and stay on course.

Regardless of what is and is not working, expect some of both and also expect to refine your plan. Avoid any thoughts that when something (and perhaps everything) you are doing did not initially work, your efforts have been in vain and there is little or no hope of success. Case in point, Edison is said to have failed 999 times before he produced a working light bulb. When asked about failing so many times he is reported to have said, "I did not fail, it just took 1,000 steps to arrive at success." This story would be a good thought to keep in mind when needing the required patience to reduce self-harming behavior with a young person.

Can the Pattern of Self-Harm be Reversed?

Self-harm is a problem behavior that can cause adults to become alarmed and then experience panic that can turn into frustration and discouragement. However, consider what has produced self-harm in the first place, and that is generally the internal stress and overwhelming concern and frustration of the young person. If the child moves from being overwhelmed to hopelessness, then suicidal behavior may be next. It is critically important that the adult does not reflect these same concerns, but instead expresses confidence and hopefulness.

One of the most positive messages coming out of brain research over the last two decades has been the concept of neuro-plasticity, or what I refer to as neuro-transformation. This concept reflects how the brain is ever changing and rebuilding itself. I don't see plastic as the best analogy for this concept because plastic can initially be molded easily, but most plastics stay rigid afterward. Neuro-transformation reflects how the brain not only changes the 'mind' (the self-aware component within the brain that is not housed in any physical structure of the brain), but also changes its physical structure as it gains experiences throughout life. Truly the brain is constantly transforming itself to better address the challenges it faces, the situations it encounters, and the successes and failures of how it responds.

Neuro-transformation alone provides more than enough evidence that self-harm and NSSI can be reversed with persistence and the right prescription for the true problem(s) behind the behavior. Although the brain has the capacity to adjust in an adaptive manner to challenging situations, the young person's mind may need to rely initially on the confidence and hopefulness of a caring adult. Therefore, it is important that the child see reflected in the verbal and non-verbal messages of adults that together we will get beyond this problem, and there will be better days ahead that do not include self-harming behavior. As the young person gains confidence from: first having a plan, second feeling the support of helpful adults, and third feeling some success, the confidence can be internalized because the human brain wants to thrive and wants to succeed if it perceives a path to do so.

Outward and inward aggression are often linked.

Angry and aggressive children act out in violence more than adults or teens. This behavior is often an indicator of the pain within. It is also frequently the case where violent acts toward others are only one form of the aggression, with self-harm being the other outlet. It is critical to understand angry, aggressive children when they are young because aggression like many other behaviors can become habitual and lead to antisocial and even criminal behavior later in life. These children can be helped to break patterns of aggression while young—and the earlier the better.

Helpful and Unhelpful Interventions

Essentially every intervention for self-harm will fall somewhere on the continuum between effective to ineffective, and even the effective ones will need adjustments. However, some interventions are much more likely to work than others; for example interventions that meet the RELIEF standard will be more effective. To predict in advance what has the best chance of success, the Royal College of Psychiatrists (2014) in the United Kingdom has the following suggestions:

Do:

- *Talk to the individual when he or she feels like self-harming. Try to understand the young person's feelings, and then move the conversation onto other things.*
- *Take some of the mystery out of self-harm by helping the individual find out about self-harm, perhaps by providing information, or by using the internet or the local library.*
- *Find out about getting help - consider going with the young person to see someone, such as their medical or psychological provider.*
- *Help the young person think about self-harming behavior not as a shameful secret, but as a problem to be sorted out.*

Don't:

- *Try to be a therapist you are not – therapy is complicated and you have enough to deal with as the child's parent, teacher or coach.*
- *Get in a hurry and expect the young person to stop overnight – it's difficult and takes time and effort.*
- *React with strong words and emotions like anger, hurt, or frustration - this can add to the problem and make it worse. Talk honestly about the effect the self-harm has on you, but do this calmly and in a way that shows how much you care for the young person.*
- *Power struggle with the young person when about to self-harm – it's better to walk away and to suggest the individual come and talk about it rather than do it.*
- *Expect a promise not to do it again – promises are seldom effective.*
- *Give the message you will distance yourself if the self-harm does not stop.*

- *Take responsibility for the self-harm and don't think it is solely your job to stop the behavior. You want to help but you must also handle your own stress, which includes the young person's self-harming behavior. Make sure you talk to your support system and take care of yourself. Be a good role model for coping with a difficult situation.*

[For more information go to the website www.rcpsych.ac.uk]

When to Get Help and Where to Find It

The point has already been made that for traumatized young people it is a very good idea to include professional help in the form of trauma treatment. Most trauma experts consider it a very good idea to provide all children with some form of therapeutic help for past trauma. One of many reasons for this is the potential long-term impact trauma has on the brain, and this results in the young person's stress and reactivity not getting better over time, but often getting worse. With the right help early on, the negative impacts of trauma can be mitigated and the earlier the better for the brain and for the child's quality of life.

When it is time to obtain professional help, not all professionals are equal. Both the credentials and the person are both important factors. It is best to begin with the professional discipline. Do you approach a psychiatrist (a medical doctor with medication training) or a psychologist (a psychological doctor with training in psychotherapy) or a clinical social worker, family therapist, or child development professional? All potentially have something to offer for addressing self-harm. How you decide may be influenced by who is available in your vicinity, or by who may be covered by health insurance. If you don't know what discipline to pursue, it may help to call your local mental health authority, which you should be able to find in the phone book or internet under government organizations. Then explain the problem and ask for some local recommendations. You can then contact two other sources of potential help: a local non-profit counseling organization and a social service organization that does not offer mental health counseling (to obtain an objective opinion). In each call briefly mention what you are looking for—"I am trying to find a professional to help me with my daughter who is struggling with her traumatic childhood and has been harming herself, could you please give me three resources you recommend." After you have talked to everyone, see what names or resources come up more than once in your conversations.

The internet offers considerable information on resources. You can do a search for psychiatrists/psychologists/therapists who have advertised expertise in trauma or child and adolescent treatment. Keep in mind that anyone can have an impressive website, but it is the individual not the website that is important. When you have identified a potential resource, make an appointment and meet the person to explain what you are looking for. You must do your best in a short period of time to ask good questions to determine the experience, the expertise and the orientation of the professional. Most of all you must ask yourself, do I believe this person can help my child and help me? If the answer is no, don't go back, return to the list of referrals and try again. With persistence you can find the help that will give you and your family considerably more peace of mind going forward.

Final Thoughts

The challenge for adults, particularly parents, in facing self-harm with young people cannot be minimized. These are behaviors that can defy common sense and logic. It can seem like an impossible task to protect a child while the child is intent on self-harm. However, helping young people with self-harming behavior is not impossible, and it is essential for adults to understand this and act accordingly. Addressing all types of negative behavior involves changing perceptions, and the adult must begin with examining personal perceptions. If the adult believes the battle cannot be won, actions will follow this thinking. However, if the adult remains optimistic in the face of a daunting challenge, optimism will follow in energy and the non-verbal messages that are sent to the child. A child who is trapped in self-harm does not need further discouragement; this is a component of the problem in the first place. But it is unreasonable to expect a parent who learns about self-harm to be calm, confident and self-assured. Most parents would be alarmed and somewhere on the Richter Scale of panic; this can only be considered a normal reaction and certainly not a sign of being a poor parent. But adults will not be able to succeed in the challenge of countering an abnormal behavior by normal reactivity; it will take more, sometimes a great deal more. While difficult, everyone will agree that the goal is worth the effort.

Multiple times the point has been made that social support is the best method to manage and cope with stress. This applies to adults also. Get the support you need, get the ideas that can help you. When you have a plan, your energy can be focused and stress will naturally turn into positive steps to problem solve. The purpose of this book, the third in the Success Series, is meant to be supportive to the key element that a troubled child needs — a caring adult.

Information on NSSI has been provided throughout, and the point will be made again that you need not be an expert in self-harm, but you do need to be an expert regarding the child you are attempting to help. Several methods have been suggested, including the Neurological Reparative Therapy Intervention Protocol that you will find in the Appendix. Take advantage of these methods to develop a plan of action, stay positive, and remember the child's brain wants to thrive and only pursues self-harm due to confusion. You can help a child change perceptions, and when you do you can help a child lead a more positive and successful life. But there is one consideration that cannot be ignored by the adult, and that is—if you do not help rescue the young person from him or herself, then who will? On behalf of the child, thank you for all you do to find answers to the difficult problem of childhood self-harm.

Summary Points

➢ Self-harm can be habit forming, so the sooner it is addressed the better.

➢ Because self-harm can reduce or mask stress, the brain needs a better method to do so to eliminate the behavior.

➢ Prevention is always better than intervention, so promote resiliency in all young people.

➢ Self-harm may be obvious or it may be hidden, it may take some detective work to spot the extent and frequency.

➢ Replace NSSI with activities that better reduce overwhelming stress and enhance the young person's world.

➢ There are specific qualities of parents that are most helpful in reducing self-harming behavior, including optimism and patience.

➢ Interventions can be more successful when following a step- by-step process called the NRT Intervention Protocol.

- ➢ Make sure the intervention plan brings RELIEF to the young person.
- ➢ Self-harm can and must be reversed, and the time to do so is when the behavior first appears.
- ➢ Some Dos and Don'ts can guide adults to help prevent and eliminate self-harming behavior (see 83).
- ➢ Know when to get professional help and where to find what you need.
- ➢ To help a young person: be patient, be planful, be positive and avoid negative feelings and impatience.
- ➢ If the young person could cope with life without self-harm, he or she would — adults must find the solutions.

Appendix

Neurological Reparative Therapy Intervention Protocol

The following process can be utilized to develop interventions under the NRT model. It is designed to proceed step-by-step through the process of identifying the underlying problem by: considering the meaning of the target symptom to the child, learning what the child is actually saying to adults, considering the background causes, developing specific interventions, and ending with monitoring and adjusting interventions over time.

Step I. Define the specific target symptom to address:

- Decide where to start; you may not want to take on the biggest issue first, or you may decide to do just that.
- Choose a target symptom that can be observed and measured.
- Be specific and detailed, avoid "He is always angry," instead "He responds with intense anger when he is told he is wrong and needs to redo his school work."

Target Symptom Statement:

_____
_____
_____
_____
_____
_____
_____
_____
_____

Step II. Identify the meaning of the target symptom to the child.

   A. Translate the meaning of the behavior:
   - List the possible translations of the child's behavior; come up with at least 7 but not more than 12.
   - Make sure at least two are "thinking outside the box" translations.

_____

_____

_____

_____

_____

_____

_____

_____

_____

_____

_____

_____

[_____]

[_____]

Now have the person who best knows the child in the context of the target symptom place a "-" before the translations that do not fit, a "+" before the translations that do fit, and a "++" if the translation fits to a significant degree. Combine the endorsed translations, particularly the "++" and put the translations together to come up with the 'most likely' translation of the meaning of the behavior to the child. It may be wrong, but it will be the best educated guess.

Step II

B. Learning the meaning of the child's words related to the target symptom.

Frequent statements/Opposite meaning

_____

_____

_____

_____

_____

_____

_____

_____

_____

_____

_____

_____

_____

_____

_____

_____

_____

_____

Many children with emotional and behavioral problems speak in opposites. Rephrase the child's statements with the opposite meaning on the right side of the form. Circle which you believe to be more accurate for the child.

To complete Step II combine the most likely meaning of the target symptom with the most accurate statements. The following is the working translation of the target symptom:

_____
_____
_____
_____
_____
_____
_____
_____
_____
_____
_____

Step III. Consider causes of the target symptom.

Review the child's background with particular attention to any trauma history. Consider the perceptions of the child represented in the meaning of the behavior in Step II. What links exist between the child's history and the child's perceptions? If there are links between the two, this is likely the background cause of the target symptom. Knowing the cause provides the best likelihood of an effective intervention.

Trauma history

_____
_____
_____
_____

Family and developmental history

_____
_____
_____
_____
_____

Step IV. Develop a list of potential interventions

- Consider multiple interventions.
- Include interventions supported by the environment of the child.
- Start with a manageable number of interventions (2-5).
- Insure each intervention specifically addresses the meaning and causes of the target symptom.

_____

_____

_____

_____

_____

_____

_____

_____

_____

_____

_____

_____

_____

_____

_____

Step V. Evaluate what is and is not working with the interventions.

- Determine a timeline to assess the effectiveness of each intervention.
- Avoid putting too much faith in any one intervention.
- Do not expect to find gold in the first shovel of gravel.
- Expect to revise all interventions, even the ones that are effective; what works today may not work tomorrow.

- Even if the target symptom improves, it is likely that other target symptoms will need to be addressed. With a new target symptom begin again at Step I.
- Model to everyone in the child's world that improvement is a long process with many course corrections along the way.

References

American Foundation for Suicide Prevention. (2015). http://www.afsp.org/understanding-suicide/facts-and-figures

Barnes, P.M., Bloom, B. & Nahin, R.L. (2008). Complementary Alternative Medicine Use Among Adults and Children: United States 2007. U.S. Department of Health and Human Services, National Health Statistics Reports, 1 - 24.

Beautrais, A.L. (2003). Suicide and Serious Suicide Attempts in Youth: A Multiple-Group Comparison Study. *American Journal of Psychiatry, 160(6),* 1093-1099.

Bertolote J.M. & Fleischmann A. (2002). Suicide and psychiatric diagnosis: A worldwide perspective. *World Psychiatry, 1*(3), 181–185.

Bohanna I. & Wang X. (2012). Media guidelines for the responsible reporting of suicide: a review of effectiveness. *Crisis: Journal of Crisis Intervention & Suicide, 33*(4), 190–198.

Boudewyn, A.C. & Huser Liam, J. (1995). Childhood sexual abuse as a precursor to depression and self-destructive behavior in adulthood. *Journal of Traumatic Stress, 8,* 445-459.

Bowlby, J. (1982). *Attachment.* Basic Books Inc.: New York.

Bridge, J.A., Asti, L. Horowitz, L.M., Greenhouse, J.B., Fontanella, C.A., Sheftall, A.H., Kelleher, K.J. & Campo, J.V.

(2015). Suicide Trends Among Elementary School–Aged Children in the United States From 1993 to 2012. *The Journal of the American Medical Association Pediatrics, 169(7),* 673-677.

Brodsky, B.S., Cloitre, M. & Dulit, R.A. (1995). Relationship of dissociation to self-mutilation and childhood abuse in borderline personality disorder. *American Journal of Psychiatry, 152(12),* 1788-1792.

Calcedo, S. & Whitlock, J.L. (2009). The Fact Sheet Series, Cornell Research Program on Self-Injury and Recovery. Cornell University: Ithaca, NY.

Copeland W.E., Angold A., Costello E.J. & Egger H. (2013). Prevalence, comorbidity, and correlates of DSM-5 proposed disruptive mood dysregulation disorder. *American Journal of Psychiatry, 170,* 173–179.

de Leo D. & Heller T. (2008). Social modeling in the transmission of suicidality. *Crisis: Journal of Crisis Intervention & Suicide, 29(1),* 11–19.

Dubo, E.D., Zanarini, M.C. Lewis, R.E. & Williams, A.A. (1997). Childhood antecedents to self-destructiveness in borderline personality disorder. *Canadian Journal of Psychiatry, 42,* 63-69.

Felitti, V.J., Anda, R.F., Nordenberg, D., Williamson, D.F., Spitz, A.M., Edwards, V. & Koss, M.P. (1998). The Relationship of Adult Health Status to Childhood Abuse and

Household Dysfunction. *American Journal of Preventive Medicine, 14,* 245-258.

Garfinkel, D., Froese, A. & Hood, J. (1982). Suicide attempts on children and adolescents. *American Journal of Psychiatry, 139 (10),* 1257-1261.

Hawton K., Fagg J., Simkin S., Bale E. & Bond A.J. (2000). Deliberate Self-Harm in Adolescents in Oxford, 1985-1995. *Journal of Adolescents, 23(1),* 47-55.

Holder, M., Coleman, B. & Wallace, J. (2008) Spirituality, Religiousness, and Happiness in Children Aged 8–12 Years. *Journal of Happiness Studies,11(2), 131-150.*

Jason Foundation. (2015) http://jasonfoundation.com/youth-suicide/facts-stats/.

Juel-Nielsen N. & Videbech T. (1970). A twin study of suicide. *Acta Geneticae Medicae et Gemellologiae, 19*(1), 307–310.

Klomek A.B., Kleinman, M., Altschuler, E., Marrocco, F., Amakawa, L. & Gould, M.S. (2011). High school bullying as a risk for later depression and suicidality. *Suicide and Life-Threatening Behavior, 41*(5), 501–516.

Lester D. (2002). Twin studies of suicidal behavior. *Archives of Suicide Research, 6,* 338–389.

Lim, C. & Putnam, R. (2010). Religion, Social Networks, and Life Satisfaction. *American Sociological Review 75(6),* 914-933.

Low, G., Jones, D., MacLeod, A., Power, M. & Duggan, C. (2000). Childhood trauma, dissociation and self-harming behavior: a pilot study. *British Journal of Medical Psychology, 72(2)*, 269-278.

Luoma J.B., Martin C.E. & Pearson J.L. (2002). Contact with mental health and primary care providers before suicide: A review of the evidence. *American Journal of Psychiatry, 159(6)*, 909–916.

Muehlenkamp, J.J., & Gutierrez, P.M. (2007). Risk for suicide attempts among adolescents who engage in non-suicidal self-injury. *Archives of Suicide Research, 11*, 69–82.

Nanamoli B. & Bodhi B. (1995). <u>A Translation of the Majjhima Nikaya</u>. Wisdom Publications: Somerville, MA.

Nock, M. K., Joiner, T. E., Gordon, K. H., Lloyd-Richardson, E., & Prinstein, M. J. (2006). Non-suicidal self-injury among adolescents: Diagnostic correlates and relation to suicide attempts. *Psychiatry Research, 144*, 65–72.

Noll, J.G., Horowitz, L.A., Bonanno, G.A., Trickett, P.K. & Putnam, F.W. (2003). Revictimization and self-harm in females who experienced childhood sexual abuse. *Journal of Interpersonal Violence, 18*, 1452-1471.

Obergefell v. Hodges, 570 U.S., (2015).

Ram Dass, (1979). Straight Talk with Ram Dass An Interview. *Yoga Journal*, #26.

Roy A., Segal N.L., Centerwall B.S. & Robinette C.D. (1991). Suicide in twins. *Archives of General Psychiatry, 48(1)*, 29–32.

Royal College of Psychiatrists. (2014). Self-Harm. Retrieved from http://www.rcpsych.ac.uk/healthadvice/problemsdisorders/self-harm.aspx.

Sapolsky, R. M. (2004). *Why Zebras Don't Get Ulcers*. Henry Holt and Company: New York.

Schore, A.N. (2001). The Effects of Early Relational Trauma on Right Brain Development, Affect Regulation, and Infant Mental Health. *Infant Mental Health Journal, 22(1-2)*, 201-269.

Schueller, S.M. & Seligman, M. (2010). Pursuit of pleasure, engagement, and meaning: Relationships to subjective and objective measures of well-being. *The Journal of Positive Psychology, 5(4)*, 253-263.

Shaffer, D., Gould, M.S., Fisher P., Trautman, P., Moreau, D., Kleinman, M. & Flory, M. (1996). Psychiatric Diagnosis in Child and Adolescent Suicide, *Journal of the American Medical Association, 53(4)*.

Shaunesey, K., Cohen, J.L., Plummer, B. & Berman, A. (1993). Suicidality in hospitalized adolescents: Relationship to prior abuse. *American Journal of Orthopsychiatry, 63(1)*, 113-119.

Sisask M. & Värnik A. (2012). Media roles in suicide prevention: a systematic review. *International Journal of Environmental Research and Public Health, 9(1)*, 123–138.

Tracy, B. (2003). *Change your thinking, change your life.* John Wiley and Sons: New Jersey.

van der Kolk, B.A., Perry, J.C., & Herman, J.L. (1991). Childhood origins of self-destructive behavior. *American Journal of Psychiatry, 148*, 1665–1671.

Walmsley, R. (2013). World Prison Population List (Tenth Edition). *International Centre for Prison Studies.* London, UK.

Weisz, J.R. (2014). Building Robust Psychotherapies for Children and Adolescents. *Perspectives on Psychological Science, 9*, 81-84.

Whitlock, J.L, Eckenrode, J. & Silverman, D. (2006). Self-injurious behaviors in a college population. *Pediatrics, 117.* 1939-1948.

Whitlock, J.L. & Knox, K. (2007). The relationship between suicide and self-injury in a young adult population. *Archives of Pediatrics and Adolescent Medicine, 161(7)*, 634-640.

Xu, J.Q., Kochanek, K.D., Murphy, S.L. & Arias E. (2014). Mortality in the United States, 2012. NCHS data brief, 168. National Center for Health Statistics: Hyattsville, MD.

Yates, T.M. (2004). The developmental psychopathology of self-injurious behavior: Compensatory regulation in posttraumatic adaptation. Clinical Psychology Review, *24(1)*, 35–74.

Yates, T.M. (2007). The developmental consequences of child emotional abuse: A neurodevelopmental perspective. *Journal of Emotional Abuse, 7*, 19-34.

Yates, T.M., Tracy, A.J. & Luthar, S.S. (2008). Non-suicidal self-injury among "privileged" youth: Longitudinal and cross-sectional approaches to developmental process. *Journal of Consulting and Clinical Psychology, 76*, 52-62.

Yip P.S., Caine E., Yousuf S., Chang S.S., Wu K.C. & Chen Y.Y. (2012). Means restriction for suicide prevention. *Lancet, 379*(9834), 2393–2399.

Ziegler, D.L. (2005). *Achieving Success with Impossible Children, How to Win the Battle of Wills.* Acacia Publishing: Phoenix.

Ziegler, D.L. (2011). *Traumatic Experience and the Brain, A Handbook for Understanding and Treating Those Traumatized as Children, Second Edition.* Acacia Publishing: Phoenix.

Ziegler, D.L. (2011). *Neurological Reparative Therapy, a Roadmap to Healing, Resiliency and Well-Being.* Jasper Mountain: Jasper, Oregon.

Ziegler, D.L. (2012). Childlike Play is Affected by Traumatic Experience. Jasper Mountain, Oregon. jaspermountain.org/childlike_play_traumatic_experience.pdf.